WITNESS

ROBERT RIENT

FRANK GARRETT
TRANS.

Happy Birthday,
Michael – Today &
every day.

–Frank

Outpost19 | San Francisco
outpost19.com

Witness Copyright 2016 by Robert Rient
Translation Copyright 2016 by Frank Garrett
Published 2016 by Outpost19
All rights reserved

ISBN: 9781944853051 (pbk)

Library of Congress Control Number: 2016916438

OUTPOST19

ORIGINAL
PROVOCATIVE
READING

Witness is the story of a boy named Luke who became a man named Robert. They take turns telling their story, with a third voice explaining the beliefs and practices of Jehovah Witnesses, the religion they escaped. *Witness* was published in Poland in May 2015. A pronunciation guide to key words left in Polish is at the back of the book, following the original text.

WITNESS

ROBERT RIENT

FRANK GARRETT
TRANS.

to Ewelina and Luke

And if there, where you were before you had started to go,
a light was burning in the windows,
from here you would no longer see it.
—Natalia de Barbaro, *Darkroom*

Luke

My first memory is a fire that went up in a flash. It's a frightening memory, and the fear will return later. And my mom, who didn't know about the fire yet, went out in front of the house, glad that at the neighbors' it's also dark. At six the power was out probably due to the November wind. My dad, who had brought back some cabbage, didn't know about it. They lit candles. They shredded the cabbage and threw it in a metal tub. Me and my brother, who also didn't know anything about the fire, climbed into the tub onto the shredded cabbage to press it. We giggled. Once a year you get to stomp cabbage barefoot.

For dinner there's rice with thawed-out strawberries and cream. Mama carries two plates in her hand. She carries two plates and a candle and calls out to her parents, calls out to them like this, "Food, grandma. Grandpa, food!" Grandma just came back from the store. She sticks the receipts in a notebook. In those days everything was on paper receipts and balancing the budget was done daily. Mama leaves the plates and goes back. She sees a light through the door with rippled glass that leads to the upstairs and she thinks that maybe the power's already come back on. She opens the door. Just then the fire flares up.

Afterwards each of us will hear countless times: You were lucky it was in the evening and not at night. Because sometimes you manage to sleep through a fire.

Mama and grandma run to the nearest neighbor a little more than 200 yards away. They had to call the fire department.

"Why did the both of you run?"

Mama turns around and sees that the flames had gone through the shingles on the roof. In the attic there was hay for the cows that had to last all winter. Grandpa says there was five tons of hay. The paper and illegal printing press had been removed from the attic a few months earlier. Now beneath the wooden ceiling there was just hay, a recently bought aluminum radiator, and a circuit breaker. The first spark must've jumped there, as determined by the Polish National Insurance. A wire inside the circuit overheated.

In the *Jelenia Góra News* the next day they wrote that there was a big power surge and that in some houses the television sets busted, lightbulbs cracked. But despite all that, people held on to their own view—that we had intentionally started the fire in order to get the insurance money. And that the greenbacks flew through the air from Brooklyn. The firemen had for sure been looking for these dollars instead of putting out the fire.

I bolt and almost succeed in getting away. Nobody knows where I'm running to, only that I'm running from the fire. My brother catches up with me and then my mom. She snatches me up and the three of us go back to the burning house. From now on I'll remember only these few minutes. But

I will remember.

They sit me down in an armchair carried from the burning house. They cover me with blankets. It's November 4, 1984, and it had just gotten dark. As I'd like to remember it, there had to have been almost twenty blankets. But I know I'm exaggerating. And I can't move. I watch the house burn.

In her hands mom is holding a hose connected to the faucet. She stands on the other side of the door with rippled glass and sprays water on the stairs that lead to the second floor. Chips of cheap paint from the wood paneling are falling on her hands and face. Somewhere they must've exposed the electrical wires because every now and then I feel a tingle on my hands.

Meanwhile dad had managed to fall down several times. To this day he has the marks of those accidents on his shins—from shelves, bookcases, cabinets. Running on slippery linoleum to the window and back. Everything he grabs he throws outside.

"I'll just have to clean it!" mom shouts and throws back through the window what dad had thrown out.

"The house is on fire!" he replies.

For a moment she's still throwing clothes and blankets into the burning house. Then she stops.

I see this clearly. I'm sitting in the armchair. I'm four years old and I see it all.

I really like this story. We often repeat it during

family gatherings. And still, even as I'm running and almost make it to the neighbors', my brother catches me. But most of all, how mom is throwing blankets and clothes—good, unburned blankets and clothes—back into our burning house.

More and more people show up. Some line up and pass various things from hand to hand, things from the house. Others stand next to me and watch. Grandpa remembers how he rescued a couple of car tires and a leather bag. He handed them to someone. Neither tires nor bag were ever found. It was dark. The firefighters had warned us.

At this point my parents aren't thinking about documents, only shouting that the house was on fire. They'll talk about this for a long time, that they should've first taken the documents. A few months later I'll get a used black briefcase that you can lock with a code. It'll lay under my bed or next to my desk in order to be close at hand if I need to make a run for it. It needs to fit what would be impossible to go on living without. In grade school there'll be letters, magnetic stripe cards, almost four hundred of them. And the most important notebook, the one with a gray cover and my poetry. In high school I'll wear out the inside pocket from one side where I'll keep my porno mags. Until now only me and God knew about this. Later, still more letters, newspapers, and a Bible will make an appearance in it.

Finally the firefighters arrive, without water. And

since the nearest fire hydrants are too grimy they drive almost four miles away to Piechowice to fill their tanks. They return to douse what had burned, the roof, the upstairs. Almost nothing was left. Brick walls, black doorframes, shattered glass.

The ceiling over the ground floor hadn't collapsed. The firefighters walk around there with flashlights.

"What are you doing?"

"We're finishing our inspection."

In the kitchen was a sugar bowl and inside it were gold wedding rings. In the morning my parents found the sugar bowl empty on the floor. And as Grandpa Janek, dad's father, arrived by train, he carried clothes under his arm because he had recognized somewhere a skirt and the cotton blouse with a collar he had once seen mom in. A few days later they found a decanter in the shape of a fish and a set of glasses. Someone was selling their set on the sidewalk in town.

Others make themselves useful. Brother Zenek pulls up in his Maluch, a little Polish Fiat 126p. He carries me and my brother and mom to Nel's, dad's sister's. Mom rushes through the foyer. She has to use the toilet. In the bathroom she looks in the mirror. She doesn't see her face, only black splotches. She starts to cry and can't stop. We stay at my aunt's, but she goes back with Brother Zenek to keep an eye on the house. The firefighters warned us. In the cellar are enough potatoes for the entire winter and cabbage. Everything is flooded though still salvageable. It'd be a shame if someone took them.

The four of them sleep in the Maluch. Zenek, grandpa, mom, and dad, who remembers the sound of the heater. They had it in the car. They pulled the extension cord all the way from the house. They kept it on since it was getting cold. From that night dad will remember only the sound of the heater.

We were given two rooms at the Lily of the Valley, a recreation center for the Workers' Holiday Fund. A shared kitchen and bathroom and these two rooms. In one, grandma and grandpa. In the other, dad, mom, my brother, and me. Grandpa didn't want to live in Szklarska Poręba any longer. He found some shack in Posada and more than seven acres of land. He and grandma moved about forty miles to the west.

Brothers and sisters helped us out. They prayed for us, shared food and clothes. Sister Hellerowa from Germany sent three blue metal barrels full of sweets and secondhand clothes.

Eventually my parents rented two rooms with a kitchen in an educational center, on the fourth floor. A few years back I went to check because I always thought it was the eleventh floor. Or maybe the eighth. I remember well how high it was. Mom had gone out for bread. I stayed at home alone with the fire. My body sank into trembles and tears. I leaned out the window and yelled.

"There'll be a fire!"

"No there won't."

"What if there is?"

"Run down the stairs."

"I won't have time. They'll burn too."

At night the siren of a fire engine woke us up. Somebody had torched their neighbor's barn. Corn, hay, pigs, and chickens burned. That same winter in Lower Szklarska Poręba on ul. Wiejska a siren also wailed. They took off, mom and dad. Now whenever a siren wailed, they ran. A big house, a former state-owned resort that had been converted to private property. They lowered the kids from the fourth floor in blankets. Some man remembered his money. They stopped him, but he kept screaming that he had to go back in. He started to crawl through the window. They pulled him back but he managed to get away. He didn't survive.

Robert

Part of the left wall built with Prussian brick still stands where the kitchen was. Nettles and wild raspberries have taken over the entrance to the basement. There's also one window. Through it you can see birch saplings growing out of the floor of what used to be the guest room. For thirty years only time has laid waste to the burned out house. While nearby, a little more than twenty yards away, stands a new house where his parents live.

The black briefcase full of letters has weathered twenty-one changes of address. And not a single fire. I take it out of the closet. One latch is broken.

The other, locked with a code. I try 919. It works. He told me once that he had forgotten the number sequence and had to try 918 times before he was successful. Since then the combination hasn't changed.

I open it. It smells musty, like a basement, like parched paper. Inside the letters are organized according to sender. And a notebook with a gray cover. That's how we met in 1991. We were little more than eleven years old. He handed me the notebook, a pen. I wrote him a poem, rhymed. He smiled. And then he told me to leave.

I suppose we already knew then that we would meet again and that I would have to live. That he had to die. I didn't kill him. But had he not died, I wouldn't have been. Everything that happened to him, every torment, was convenient for me. His weakness and self-loathing were my justification and my provocation. Besides, he wanted to die. He talked about it again and again. I have evidence. I am the witness regarding this matter.

Luke

We lived in a new house made of gray cinder blocks. My dad poured them one by one. The ruins of the burned house were a playground until the roof collapsed. They briefly served as a chicken coop.

From the window of my room I have a view of the charred rubble. On sunny days it's enough to lean out a little and look to the left to catch sight of the peak of Szrenica.

The fact that I'm different I learn in kindergarten.

The day before September 1 I make myself a diaper out of crumpled up rolls of toilet paper. This solves nothing. The next night I wet the bed.

I don't like to walk almost two miles one-way and stay away from home for long. Alone with strangers. I had gotten used to mom. To her workshop with a floor full of colorful threads and the sound of her sewing machine.

Today for Grandmothers' Day we're all making cards. I couldn't finish because in addition to Dziunia, mom's mother, and Marta, dad's mother, there's still Grandma Kazia, Pela, Marysia, Helena, Adela, Józia, and Wala. Everyone makes one card or two but I have to make nine.

My elementary school is closer than kindergarten was. It takes half an hour. Uphill or downhill, because that's how you walk in Szklarska Poręba. Sometimes an hour or more, if a roundabout way with adventures is chosen. The forest, a roadway over the railroad tracks, and underpasses. A stream with calamus. A clearing. Two escarpments. In winter, snowdrifts. Burying under the snow. In the middle of a dirt road, dog poop. And once it was even my own, so that somebody could step in it. Building snowmen. Knocking the snow down from the trees with one kick and a speedy getaway. From school most walk to the right, to Upper Szklarska, but a few, like me, to Central.

I'm sitting in art class drawing a flower. I try to

hide it on the sheet of paper, to cover up my flower. To use two colors like everybody else coloring the flag. I'm not allowed. I know this much. A classmate next to me asks why I'm drawing something else. This moment is the worst. End of assignment. All the works are hanging on the chalkboard so you can admire them. There are around twenty Polish flags. And one flower. This moment is the worst.

After a few months everyone in class will already know about me being different. After several years most will be used to it.

At assembly during the national anthem I sometimes stand, though I should sit. But the crowd excites me. They're watching me, I think. I feel the gaze of my classmates, the teachers, and principal. Even though I'm looking at the floor. I don't sing, ever. In the older grades some people also don't sing, but it's those who sit at the back of the bleachers, who are in charge. Who I'll never belong to. I'm learning all too well. I am, after all, of the feline faith.

The worst are birthdays and name days. Every couple of weeks somebody's celebrating one. I had a dream that all the birthdays and name days were in July and August. Then I'd have peace of mind. It's all about the sweets. Whoever has a birthday isn't prompted. In class, best if it's chemistry or math, the birthday kid goes row by row handing out candy. He puts his hand into a brown paper bag. Everybody takes one. I don't take the candy, don't offer wishes. Then, not always but usually, the class sings "*Sto lat*," wishing the birthday kid a long life of a hundred years. I don't sing. If someone has a lot of candy, he passes it out in every class, which everybody enjoys, though I'd prefer a spelling quiz. Some come up next to me with their bag full of candy and don't pause, don't pressure. It is after all just candy. Others look offended or ask why, if I don't like them. Yeah, but why? Because I don't celebrate. Because we give each other presents all year long. Yeah, but it's candy. No, because I don't celebrate. Those few seconds, in which I don't know what to do with myself, with my hands, with my eyes, are the worst. I don't know what to do with my sense of guilt before the class, before all those I want to be liked by. I don't know what to do with the shame. Jesus, for sure, wouldn't have been ashamed. He'd look straight ahead with pride and wouldn't worry about anything. Just like Shadrach, Meshach, and Abednego who didn't bow before the statue.

A long time ago in Babylon King Nebuchadnezzar built an enormous golden statue. And he said that whoever doesn't bow to it "will at the same moment be thrown into the burning fiery furnace" (Dan 3:6). Shadrach, Meshach, and Abednego, Jewish servants of Jehovah, didn't worship it. They even said to the king that if God wills, he will deliver them. And even if He doesn't, they'd prefer to die regardless. Nebuchadnezzar was furious. He ordered the furnace to be heated seven times hotter and to have Shadrach, Meshach, and Abednego tossed in. Then there appeared an angel among them. And the fire did not consume them.

This story comes from the 1981 book *My Collection of Bible Stories* that my parents read to me for as long as I can remember. In the drawing you can see three proud men and behind them the crowd bowing before the statue. I know this drawing well. I know Shadrach, Meshach, and Abednego well. They have no shame or pangs of guilt. And I only have to refuse candy, nothing more. No fiery furnace. The worst part is that for the eight years of elementary school I want to take the candy.

I divide my teachers into the indifferent, the hostile, and the friendly.

The majority are indifferent. The lady from chemistry, art, the man from physics, math. They treat me like everyone else in class.

The minority are hostile. The lady from history, for example. I submit a draft of my report. It's worth doing. You can get an A and improve your grade at the end of the year. I talk about the life of Alexander the Great. When I mention Jesus Christ and call him the greatest of all people, she interrupts me, tells me to sit down. To stop preaching . There won't be any A's. It's humiliating. I used a textbook from school and a book from the Jehovah's Witnesses called *The Greatest Man Who Ever Lived* from 1991. At our meeting they distinctly said that in every possible situation you should bear witness to the truth. I'm scared. I don't want to. But what was I supposed to do with such a thought once it had already been thought, once Jehovah had seen it? I had to write about Jesus in my report in order to bear witness to the truth. I tell my parents how she interrupted me. I talk about it at the hall. I talk about my ordeal. This is pride.

The man from music is the friendly one, my homeroom teacher. He doesn't make me sing carols. I don't have to learn other songs. I can sit by myself and listen. And if I want to join in, I can. I never do but I appreciate it.

And what's more—that thorn in my flesh.

Robert

In adulthood he dreamed that he was walking down the empty hallways of the elementary school or that he was sitting at his desk, meeting with his friends. These dreams returned to him every few months. If you'd be so kind:

"Tell me."

"Ordinary dreams," he said with a smile.

"You mean good?

"No."

"Then what kind? Tell me."

"Not good. But not nightmares."

"Well, then what kind?"

"Ordinary dreams. About longing."

For many years I couldn't understand him. I believed that I'd never be free from what I didn't understand. And I really wanted to rid myself of him. After the initial curiosity came contempt and hatred. I wished him dead. I fell in love with him later when he began to leave. Love came without the slightest effort when I understood. That's why I write.

Witnesses

Jehovah's Witnesses don't celebrate birthdays or name days. There are two murders written about in the Bible that serve as the reason. The first was committed during Pharaoh's birthday. During the feast he had the chief of the bakers brought from prison and hanged (Gen 40:20-22). The second one happened when the daughter of Herodias danced while celebrating Herod's birthday. She pleased him so much that he promised to give her anything she asked for. She wanted the head of John the Baptist (Mt 14:6-10).

Everything that Jehovah's Witnesses believe is based on their interpretation of Holy Scripture.

On July 1, 1879, twenty-seven-year-old pastor Charles Taze Russell released in the United States the first issue of *The Watchtower*. This date is considered the beginning of the existence of the Jehovah's Witnesses organization, and Russell became its first president.

Great-grandfather Thomas brought the truth to their family when he arrived from Argentina. He was a blacksmith, a master of his trade, and also a missionary and scholar of the Holy Scripture. When he came on his visits to Poland he was in the habit of making another baby and then returning. (He died fifteen years before Luke was born.)

The current name, Jehovah's Witnesses, was adopted in 1931. Three years later, on October 7, 1934, Adolf Hitler is reported to have said in Berlin, "I will eradicate this rabble from Germany."

Purple triangles were reserved for them in the concentration camps. Signing a statement renouncing your religion and declaring loyalty to the National Socialist state generally made it possible to be released from the camp. A great many didn't sign. They didn't want to use the greeting "Heil Hitler." They refused to show reverence toward the flag or other Nazi symbols, repeating after Jesus, "My kingdom is no part of this world" (Jn 18:36).

Rudolf Höss, the commandant of the concentration camp Auschwitz, boasted in his autobiography that he knew "many religious fanatics ... on pilgrimages, in monasteries, in Palestine, on the Hejaz road in Iraq, and in Armenia. They were Catholics, both Roman and Orthodox, Moslems, Shiites and Sunnis. But the Witnesses in Sachsenhausen, and particularly two of them, surpassed anything that I had previously seen. These two especially fanatical Witnesses refused to do any work that had any connection whatever with military matters. They would not stand at attention, or drill in time with the rest, or lay their hands along the seam of their trousers, or remove their caps. They said that such marks of respect were due only to Jehovah and not to man. They recognised only one lord and master, Jehovah." They were sentenced to death. Before their execution, they weren't tied up so that they could clasp their hands together in prayer.

As the founder of their own religion, Jehovah's Witnesses recognize Jesus Christ, though they claim that it was Abel, the son of Adam and Eve, who was the first one of them. They also include Noah, Job, Abraham, and Moses in this group.

They are currently in 239 countries. They number more than eight million, of which over 123,000 live in Poland.

The *Yearbook of Jehovah's Witnesses* for 2015 reports that 275,571 new followers were baptized in the previous year. The number of disfellowshipped from the organization and of those who have left is unknown. For many years the growth rate of the faithful in Poland, as in many countries of Western Europe, has stayed at zero or minus one.

The activities of Witnesses are restricted by law or banned in many communist and Muslim countries.

According to the teaching of *The Watchtower*, nations are the work of Satan. The Kingdom of God will replace them soon. Witnesses do not salute flags, do not recognize the emblem and other symbols of the state, do not work in the police force, the city police, state offices and departments, do not engage in politics, do not go to the polls. They do not comply with the law of any country if it is contrary to the teachings of Jehovah.

"You must not murder" from the Hebrew Scriptures, strengthened with "Love your neighbor as yourself" from the Christian Greek Scriptures is sufficient reason to forgo military service.

My Parents

The first night in prison my dad couldn't fall asleep. In his cell there were eight or ten. He no longer remembers. They lay side by side, each had his own blanket. His cramped, hard bunk made of boards, as well as his headrest. Every so often one guy vomited. Nobody came for him until morning even though they all shouted. Dad didn't sleep because of the guy who vomited every so often.

When he was nineteen he was drafted into the army. He refused. He wound up being imprisoned in Wrocław, at Świebodzka 1, a closed unit. He worked as a flunky, doing menial tasks. He distributed meals, washed the floors, corridors, cleaned up. His trial took place after a month. Like the other nine on trial that day, he was assigned a public defender. He refused. He tried to explain that "all those who take the sword will perish by the sword" (Mt 26:52). He received three years; the others, two and a half each.

He wound up in the prison on Fiołkowa in an

open unit together with Marek, Piotr, and other brothers. There were also politicians, soldiers, petty thieves—all with light sentences. Even though there were twelve or sixteen of them in the cell—he no longer remembers—the bedbugs bit only him. Mostly on the elbows and neck.

Jehovah's Witnesses were given rather cushy jobs, he recalls. Marek was an electrician. Every couple of minutes they were summoning him somewhere. The other brother, a tailor, altered their trousers for them into slim, fashionable ones. In those days everyone was given baggy ones. And my dad became the supervisor of the uniform warehouse. He inspected packages for the convicts. He issued clothes. And he painted cars. By profession he was a spray painter. They liked him. One time he found fifty złoty in the crease of some trousers belonging to one of the convicts who used peddler's French. He returned it to the trousers' owner. For ten złoty you could buy a box of Madras tea. If you suffused it with a gallon of water, you'd have very strong tea. On Fiołkowa there were frequent bribes. They called them *Madras rain*. Tea trickled from behind the wall. The prisoners who used peddler's French, sometimes together with the guards, grabbed the others' packages and took off.

Thanks to this warehouse they had the latest books and newspapers, all the literature. They kept it in their clothes. The director knew. He turned a blind eye.

In the food packages that my mom brought dad

were a number of *Watchtowers* hidden at the very bottom, beneath the spreadable lard. The guards didn't bother to check. But they were young, in love. They wrote letters to each other. Between visits every few weeks. That was all they had. Mom wrote long letters. For one of dad's, sometimes three arrived. Sixteen-paged. Eventually, the unit warden flew into a rage. He doesn't have time to read this, he said. Regulations prohibit such long letters. He didn't prohibit them, but each letter had to be opened and labeled "censored."

Sometimes at morning roll call some guard would tease my dad or another brother by asking when Armageddon was coming. He'd laugh, nudging the prisoner. Well, tell us when the end of the world will be. We have to get ready.

They were lucky because there were only Jehovah's Witnesses in the cell. They organized meetings. Sometimes my dad led them. They met in various places where they could stay for longer. They prayed, sang, studied the Bible. It was clear to them that they had to sit in prison because they wouldn't learn how to kill. No government in the world could make them take part in any war. They waited for the time when Jehovah "will certainly render judgment among the nations and set matters straight respecting many peoples. And they will have to beat their swords into plowshares and their spears into pruning shears. Nation will not lift up sword against nation, neither will they learn war anymore" (Isa 2:4).

My parents' account of their first meeting:

-Yes, I remember. He was standing against the wall, a tall auburn-haired guy. A smooth talker. Witty. I liked him. Such a hotshot. That was before the pioneer center in Sobieszów.

-The first time? At the center. No, earlier. In Sobieszów, at the organizational meeting. She liked that I was handsome, a hotshot. Did she tell you that her boyfriend Tadeusz was also there?

-There was no boyfriend. We wrote letters to each other. We set up a plan that we'd get to know each other better at the center. He was a pioneer. He impressed me with his knowledge. Oh, and he wooed me.

Chromów, Lubuskie Province, 1973. Forty young people arrive at the pioneer center, including him and her. They live at Aunt Hela's. A cottage, a farm, and a shed with hay where you could sleep. Every day they head out in pairs for field service, to preach the truth from house to house. Sometimes someone reports them to the police, sics a dog on them. Arrests rarely occur. Following a brief exchange, most shut the door with disdain. As it is to this day. The center is led by Piotr, her brother, who later will also wind up in prison.

-He arrived by motorcycle.

-My mom bought the motorcycle in the GDR for 3,350 marks. She saved for years. We were freaking out at the center. I remember deep sand. I was riding it. We flipped it.

-We got up early. There was a list, who goes

with who to preach and to which village. To Krosno Odrzańskie, Lubsko, or even further. In the evening I told Piotr to assign me with him. I wanted to chat. I wake up in the morning—and we're on the list. After that, I asked again. He arranged it. Well, after a few days I went to Piotr one more time. He laughed but he agreed. At that time eight other married couples just like us got to know each other there.

-Crazy. So bonkers. Pigheaded. She did what she wanted. Before leaving for service we once smeared ourselves with paste. Once we soaked ourselves with perfume. That's when Tadeusz moved on to Ania.

-Tadeusz? He had started to bug me. He was upset like I had come with him and owed him something. I stopped liking him. Introvert, unfunny. So particular. After the center I went to Rybarzowice. Mama called, that a postcard arrived. I boarded the bus and went back.

-I had arrived on a motorcycle. A cow knocked it over, but it still worked. And after, I was always riding back and forth.

-When he went to prison, I learned how to kill chickens for him. I took him a roasted one for visitation, because he liked it. My dad didn't kill, neither did my mom. So I went to my grandma's with a live chicken. I was getting pissed off because it took a while. And then you still had to scald and pluck it. Once I got hold of the chicken I had to walk to my grandma's. But I went back for the ax. I lined it up. Once, twice, three times. I was scared. You had to grip two wings, the two claws. I finally killed it.

"Darling. The only thing left for me to do is to dream about everything, to dream about what we did, how we spent our free moments, and about what our future will be in a few years. I'm sure to change, because I already see that I'm different. Don't think too much. And keep perspective. Try to get me a picture of you."–*Censored November 25, 1973*.

"Dearest! From the second story of the courthouse, from the hallway, you could get a good view of the windows of the prison cells. What good are words here when everything is so cruel. Without the light of day, without door handles, cut off from normal life, a person is helpless, powerless. And yet the awareness that behind the wall is freedom. One would like to cry out against injustice, cruel nightmare, something that will always be buried in us. But we know the truth and we know that someday we, too, will be completely happy. You know?"–*Censored December 15, 1973*.

"So, are you really mine, can you be any more mine? I said at most a third of what I wanted to."–*Censored January 3, 1974*.

"My lovely, darling, write, please, about everything. When you get up, what you do, when you go to sleep, what you talk about, what you wear, if you're cold or not—write everything. Write something about me. I mean whether you believe me and if you let your thoughts belong to me. I want to have the right to your dreams and thoughts. Maybe it's wrong, but what to do. I love you so much, like nobody ever loved anyone."–

Censored January 5, 1974.

"Help me. I felt stupid, maybe because it's the first visit. You acted ... I didn't understand you."–*Censored January 15, 1974.*

"Help me. I can't live among people. Every discussion upsets me. I'm temperamental like never before. During the visit I was the happiest man because I had seen you. I was simply scared. I haven't stopped thinking about you. That's one topic that will never be exhausted. I get up at five o'clock at roll call, and then we go for breakfast. We must reject all the bad thoughts that Satan sends us. In the Letter to the Ephesians 4:27 it's written not to give the Devil a place! I love you. Yours."–*Censored January 19, 1974.*

"In Szklarska winter is in full swing. In a field I wrote your name in the snow. Capital letters almost fifty feet tall. I was feeling horrible. I'm desperate without you. But it'll be wonderful yet—right? Think often of the Creator. We must strive to ensure that our consciences were founded upon and brought up in the Word of God. Yours."–*Censored February 8, 1974.*

"Darling. I feel sorry for us. Life is pulsating. We have to fight it."–*Censored February 23, 1974.*

"You know what I really don't like? Blank pages in a letter. Yours."–*Censored February 25, 1974.*

"It's terrible because they also locked up my brother Piotr. It's as hard for him as it was for you and for all of you. Did you know that he's anemic? It's a vitamin deficiency. I suppose you'll get this letter also on Thursday, maybe at roll call. Will someone make you do push-ups again? It's not fair."–*Censored March 3, 1974.*

"We'll get married. If not in this world, then on the other side of Armageddon."–*Censored March 11, 1974.*

"On our meadow the purple of crocuses. I've already discussed the truth for the umpteenth times with the entire class. They disagree, though they know next to nothing about their own religion. I don't know if I convinced even one of them that they're wrong, but some have begun to seriously think. Two of them even went to their priest to check if what I was saying was true. And he didn't even know what the word *parishioners* means."–*Censored March 26, 1974.*

"You can't imagine what happened here Easter Monday.[1] What depravity. The inmates who speak peddler's French had a chance to display their talents, to get revenge on the rest of us. If they couldn't get us with water, then they threw jars, buckets, and cups. Blood was shed. And there wasn't a single warden there at the time. They dealt with it by turning off the water in the entire place. Then again, these pagan festivities flew by without anything out of the ordinary. I'm apathetic more than anything. I'd like to be happy someday."–*Censored April 16, 1974.*

---

1 In Poland, Easter is a two-day holiday, consisting of Sunday and Monday. Easter Monday, also known as Wet Monday, *Śmigus-Dyngus*, or Dyngus Day is celebrated by boys dousing girls with water and whipping them with pussy willow branches. Sometimes the boys dress as bears, and girls can ransom themselves with painted eggs. —*Trans.*

"You know what? In order to thank you for everything you've done for me, these letters of mine aren't enough. I'd have to be on the loose right now—but there's no chance of that—and maybe I could be. I already know all the more that there's only you, no one else."–*Censored April 24, 1974*.

"You're mine (not your mom and dad's)—the best, the most handsome, the dearest, darling, my one and only, do you hear? Mine! I don't know when it started, but listen: everything that belongs to you and that reminds me of you, your notebooks, certain notes, your bed, your voice on the tape recorder, your handwriting, letters, your movements, eyes, hair, your hands, face—for me it's all beautiful. What you might call noble. I treat it like something very precious. I'd like to be a boy. I'd be such a rascal."–*Censored April 28, 1974*.

"I turned nineteen and maybe that's why I think more and more about our future. I really love you— even a little badly since I love you so desperately. I'm different from most. I like to be alone—I like my solitude more and more. Sometimes I wish I didn't have to see anyone. Not a single person. I like the night. I don't sleep. I think *I am alone—so good*. That's why I often think that it'd be better if I'd never been born. I'm only scared because I want you to always understand me."–*Censored May 7, 1974*.

"I love you. I keep everything to myself. I collect, I hoard, until my head explodes. I wish I had the same kind of personality like some of the brothers. Such happy-go-lucky guys, you know? I can't stand it, especially here. I hate introverts. They need help. Nothing's going right for me. These days are so horrible."–*Censored May 10, 1974.*

"Sometimes I'd like to blow up all the introverts. Today I wish we could play hooky and go for ice cream in Jelenia Góra. And later to Perła Zachodu."–*Censored May 12, 1974.*

"Apparently I always seem prettier when I'm coming back from seeing you."–*Censored May 30, 1974.*

In 1974 amnesty was announced in the Polish People's Republic.

Dad was released from prison on August 26, after nine months and seven days.

My parents were married a year later, on July 12, 1975. They lived in an old house that had formerly belonged to a German family when this part of Poland was still Germany. The one that later burned down. Mom sewed clothes, dad painted cars. In addition, they had a cow, some chickens, a greenhouse with lettuce, tomatoes.

One day the press coordinator in Lower Silesia visited my parents. He wanted to see the house. A large space in the attic. A basement. Far from town and neighbors. They agreed to set up an illegal printing press. Four to six people were employed on a permanent basis. Everyone slept, ate, and worked in the attic. Their family, loved ones, and acquaintances, even their brothers and sisters in the congregation weren't in the know. When someone showed up unannounced, my parents pushed a special bell. The printing press had to be shut off and come to a complete standstill. The wooden beams carried every little sound. At two, three o'clock at night a passenger car pulled up and carried off the printed literature that was then distributed to the congregations and studied during weekly meetings. Mainly *The Watchtower*, *Awake!*, and books with soft covers, all black and white. Once they brought several tons of paper. It was too much. They covered it with hay. In the morning cracks were found in the ceiling.

I was born on the first day of the last month of 1980. I was supposed to have been a girl, Marta, or at least a dog, which is what my older brother had been wishing for.

Luke

In the evening in the bathroom I practice. I place my right hand over my face, with my thumb and index finger I plug my nose. I hug my right forearm with my left. I close my eyes, gently lean back. I can't wait. I've been ready for a year.

During this time I've been meeting with the elders of the congregation who have grilled me with hundreds of questions:

"Who is the true God?

When do you find the time for prayer?

How can you protect yourself from the influence of Satan and his demons?

What is sin? How did we all become sinners?

What is death?

Who will not be resurrected from the dead and why?

What is the only Scriptural basis for divorce that frees one to remarry?

Which local food products or medical practices will you from now on avoid as a Christian?

What attitude should a Christian take toward someone who has been persuaded that a blood transfusion is necessary to save his own life or the life of a loved one?

How do you provide evidence that you love Jehovah with your whole heart and mind, with all your soul and strength?

What is the Christian view of drunkenness?

What does the Bible say about sexual immorality, which includes adultery, fornication, sexual relations with another person of the same sex, and other ungodly sexual conduct?

What kinds of pressures and temptations do you have to resist in order to establish and maintain a good relationship with Jehovah?

In God's arrangement of things, who is the "head" of the married woman?

Why should you gladly preach the good news to all the inhabitants of the territory assigned to you?"

All these questions come from the book *Organized to Do Jehovah's Will*, intended for internal use by Jehovah's Witnesses, published in 1990.

Each response must be supported with a verse from the Bible. Examinations of faith are difficult, especially when your dad and granddad are testing your knowledge. They're the only elders in town. I'm getting good at ignoring my embarrassment. We meet every couple of weeks for a few hours. I want to tell them about the thorn in my flesh, Satan's angel, but the desire is short-lived and it disappears, carrying away with it the dread it's caused me.

I turn around, squint my eyes blinded by the summer sun and look around the sections of the stadium in search of my parents. I see a yellow parasol. I rise for the song, then bow my head to pray. The almost two hundred people next to me do the same. Everyone is about to be baptized. It's not going the way I'd hoped it would.

In the sections more than ten thousand brothers and sisters sit. They hide from the glaring sun under garden tents, umbrellas, and small parasols. Once a year we meet in a dozen or so large Polish cities for a three-day assembly. Baptism is always on the program. It's mostly the children of Jehovah's Witnesses, their distant relatives, as well as people experiencing pain, illnesses, sometimes trauma, or those who have problems with addiction who get baptized. Those who need a system, instructions for what they have to do in order to achieve happiness.

The lecture begins. A brother prays for us and reminds us that soon we'll have a clean slate with Jehovah, but also at the same time Satan will learn of our existence.

I'm not afraid of Satan. Maybe just a little. I can't stand still on the hot field of the stadium. I'm too excited. Because of the clean slate I get to fill in. It's the most important day of my life.

I'm one of the youngest waiting in line for the round garden swimming pool set up in the middle of the stadium. Women and girls in swimsuits form a line to a second pool. Everyone has a towel of their own. I look around the sections, at the witnesses to my baptism. I climb the ladder into the pool. The water reaches my neck. I assume the rehearsed position. I think about John the Baptist and Jesus, about how the heavens parted when he came out of the Jordan River. The elder supports my back with one hand, takes hold of me with the other. He leans me back in a swift motion and after a moment pulls me from the water.

"We welcome our new brother."

The sky doesn't open. I feel nothing other than happiness, pride. I know, I know perfectly well that no miracle is going to happen. That it's a symbol. But I was hoping for more than happiness and pride. I want to feel the blank slate. I want to feel how Jehovah takes away everything that's bad, how he removes the thorn. At once they grab my hands. My family, cousins, several dozen people, brothers and sisters. Congratulations, a pat on the back. I'm important. Disappointment vanishes. I am important. From now on I belong to Jehovah.

On dad's side there's a sister, her husband, a boy and a girl cousin in Piechowice.

A brother, his wife, and three girl cousins in Cieplice Śląskie-Zdrój.

Another brother, his wife, a girl and boy cousin in Pasiecznik.

There was one other brother, Mirek—he drowned. And a sister, Jadzia—she died in the hospital. They are waiting for the resurrection.

Grandma and grandpa live in Jelenia Góra.

Some Sundays you can visit everyone. With cake. The adults together, the kids together. And it's always too soon to go home.

On mom's side there's a brother, his wife, a boy and girl cousin in Złotoryja.

In Bogatynia, mom's sister, her twin, her husband, two boy and two girl cousins, including Ewelina, the most important of all.

Grandma and grandpa, the ones who moved from Szklarska when our house burned down, live in Posada.

Twenty-seven people. Except for grandpa who drinks and an uncle who smokes, which disqualify them, everyone's a Jehovah's Witness. But that's only the immediate family. There are still mom's and dad's cousins and their kids, including Diana, who I was friends with. To this you can add brothers and sisters, grandmas and grandpas, aunts and uncles from the congregation. Vacations were a good time without people of the world.

I was baptized July 2, 1994, at the City Stadium in Wałbrzych. I wasn't quite fourteen. I was in a hurry. My brother was baptized when he turned eighteen.

I got my urgency from my parents, from those two lovers who already in their love letters couldn't stand introverts.

To this day when mom walks, she sprints.

Witnesses

May 12, 1989, Jehovah's Witnesses were officially registered as the Faith Association of Jehovah's Witnesses in Poland, represented by the Christian Congregation of Jehovah's Witnesses. Their activities became legal.

On the plot of land next to the burned house the Kingdom Hall of the Jehovah's Witnesses was founded. Inside there was carpeting, chairs bought from a cinema, a podium, a lectern, flowers. On the wall one quotation from the Bible that changed every year. No pictures, symbols. No altar, incense. According to the commandment: "You must not have any other gods against my face. You must not make for yourself a carved image or a form like anything that is in the heavens above or that is on the earth underneath or that is in the waters under the earth" (Ex 20:3-4). The hall was built by volunteers who came from all over Poland.

For many years there was only one elder from the congregation in Szklarska Poręba (Luke's dad)—a position comparable to that of a parish priest in the Catholic Church. In the congregation there weren't more than fifty preachers. They called themselves brothers and sisters. The whole town could see who was walking up and down the streets of the city with a *Watchtower* in hand. They called it a feline faith.

To this day they assemble in the Kingdom Hall two times a week for meetings. (In the past it was three times a week.) Entry is unrestricted. In addition to the followers, anyone interested can participate. Regular items on the agenda are song, prayer, a lecture, and reading Bible passages.

After baptism you gain new privileges (just like Luke). Operating the sound system, walking around the room with a microphone during the Q&A with the followers, reading Bible passages out loud. And later being promoted to ministerial servant and elder of the congregation.

In addition to the meetings of Jehovah's Witnesses, they meet in larger "circuit assemblies" (the circuit is more or less the size of a county) and "district assemblies" (roughly the size of the województwo, or province). At such meetings, often lasting a few days, also known as conventions, baptisms take place. Witnesses do not baptize infants since Jesus said you must first teach the would-be believer (Mt 28:19-20).

Each circuit and district has its own overseer, commonly known as a traveling brother, who, moving from congregation to congregation, manages the organization.

More and more often believers meet in halls built by themselves, but large assemblies take place in municipal stadiums, usually eagerly rented to them. The day before a convention the brothers and sisters come to clean up. They clean the toilets, wash the chairs and benches, mow the grass, sweep, paint. The same happens after assemblies. They have a habit of leaving the stadium in better shape than they found it.

This is one way of bearing witness to the truth, which is preaching with deeds, not words. In every situation, they have to remember that they are being watched and that their own behavior can either encourage or discourage people from finding the truth.

Jehovah's Witnesses live inside their own vocabulary.

"The truth" is their religion but also their way of life. You can live "in the truth" or "outside the truth." The word is used so often, with such ease, that after a few years in the organization you no longer need to question the truth. On the other side is the "world," that is, everyone outside the truth. Unclaimed territory doesn't exist.

The truth is God's. The world belongs to Satan. In the world live the "apostates," the "disfellowshipped," and people of all other faiths. A coworker, a colleague, your neighbors may be nice people, but they remain people of the world, Philistines that brothers and sisters shouldn't be friends with. "Philistines were the sworn enemies of Jehovah's people, and the satanic world has adopted a similar attitude today. But the Philistines were destroyed as a nation, and Jehovah will similarly pour out his devastating wrath on this world and its religious, political, and economic systems."

The quotation comes from the July 1, 1995 issue of *The Watchtower*, that is, "literature." All publications published by the Watch Tower Bible and Tract Society of Pennsylvania, founded by Pastor Russell, are called that. Literature also includes *Awake!*, a monthly that deals with topics such as nature, the environment, the economy, including curious facts from the world of science and mysteries of the Bible.

The monthly *The Watchtower Announcing Jehovah's Kingdom* from May 2015 was issued in an edition of 52,946,000 copies in 231 languages, while *Awake!*, from this same time, had a circulation of 51,788,000 copies in 101 languages. To this you can add *The Watchtower—Study Edition*, a separate edition for followers, in addition to books, pamphlets, tracts, thematic magazines, and copies of the Bible published in the millions. The circulation of *The Watchtower* typically exceeds forty-two million, making it the magazine with the highest circulation in the world. In second place is *Awake!* with an average run of forty-one million.

Jehovah's Witnesses should satisfy their need for reading literature with their own literature.

There exists an informal list of banned books, which includes the one you're reading, and all publications expressing negatively the topic of Jehovah's Witnesses as well as the writings of former followers. Admitting to reading them risks a "pastoral visit," a reproof, and, in extreme cases, "disfellowshiping" from the congregation. On the list of banned books you'll also find publications published by other religions and sects. A pastoral visit consists of elders from the congregation (or leaders in the given community) meeting with those who have gone astray, were maybe sinning, or had stopped preaching or attending meetings.

In big cities there are several congregations with on average about a hundred people. Besides meetings, brothers and sisters also meet at "gatherings for field service," during which they prepare for "preaching," that is, proselytizing, consisting mostly of going from house to house. "Return visits" should be made to every person who accepted some kind of publication.

A "pioneer center" (like the one where Luke's parents met) is typically a two-week trip in the summer in the countryside or where there aren't a lot of followers. A dozen or so (or several dozen) people, typically young, pack backpacks, take mats, tents, an ample supply of literature, and head out together to preach.

Jehovah's Witnesses shouldn't marry the worldly. Pioneer centers are often one of the few opportunities for them to get to know their future husband or wife in the truth and the beginning of their sex lives. For this reason, the majority of Jehovah's Witnesses enter into marriage very early, between the ages of eighteen and twenty-five.

The entirety of Poland is divided into "territories" assigned to preachers. They're given little cards, usually with a map showing the two streets in the village or three apartment blocks in the city. The preachers are responsible for the region assigned to them. They make notes:

"Apartment no. 1– closed;

no. 2– M, ~45yo, not interested bc "he's Catholic," in the apt you could hear voices of other household members;

no. 3– somebody looked through the peephole like before but didn't open door, next time come at a different time;

no. 4– F, 65yo, doesn't want visitors, don't come for 3 months, no earlier, bc she'll flip out;

no. 5– F, 40yo, no time but took *Watchtower*, *Does Satan Really Exist?*, make return visits!"

All such notes indicate the date and time of day.

Every month female and male preachers "bear fruit." They fill out special forms, sign their names, number of hours spent preaching, how much literature handed out (divided into magazines, brochures, and books), how many return visits made, how many "Bible studies" they conduct, in other words, regular meetings with those interested. All of this is called "fruit." Any person who accepts literature and who Witnesses regularly meet with for Bible study is called "interested." The goal of these joint studies is to prepare the interested for baptism.

Robert

The unwritten dictionary of Jehovah's Witnesses contains significantly more words. He made use of them quite naturally. Like a hand. They constituted a part of his tongue and backbone. His needs and dreams were built from them. The narrative constrains his thoughts and creates his emotions. It penetrates into his subconsciousness and flows from his mouth, particularly in his words. A separate set of meanings creates a system that clears the way for forming a believer and sustaining his faith. That's how this mariculture comes about, this delicate net that separates believers from the world while simultaneously forcing them to live in this world. This is sometimes called insanity.

Mariculture—fish farming in natural bodies of water. The fish are kept in huge nets resembling pockets that are anchored to the seabed. A round or rectangular frame, at one time of bamboo, now made of plastic, supports it on the surface.

Fish from the mariculture have never experienced life outside the net. Perhaps they've seen the shadow of a shark or eavesdropped on fishers as they talked about dangerous storms, sea monsters, dark abysses, and dark demons ruled by Poseidon himself. Besides being afraid—all were afraid, and the fears were much too large for such small bodies—they were left to create projections of their fears. Monumental projections lying in wait for them, swimming just past the protective net. The suffering of their parents, just like their own suffering, was evidence and confirmation of the uniqueness of the situation in which they'd found themselves. They had been chosen for service. From hope arose projections of the gods who will wipe out the entire world threatening them and will rescue the brave fish huddled together in the mariculture.

It's understood that conversations with other fish, those outside the net, must result in suffering. Their audacious tales about coral reefs, the seabed full of sand, races among the rocks, or lazy drifting right in the warm sunshine of the water's expanse. Instead of listening and suffering, it's better to recognize that they're lying. Fish from the mariculture believe in the net protecting them against the evil world that goes on endlessly. They are not to be blamed for their ignorance. It wasn't them who built the net. The fish from the mariculture believe in God. Maybe without this faith they'd go crazy.

Luke

"What's this?"

"For the hospital. In case of an emergency."

"But-?"

"A declaration."

"No blood? Show me."

I pull out from my wallet a white card, folded. I won't deny Jehovah, for sure.

It was going to be different. I had promised myself that in high school it was now going to be different, that I wasn't going to be a screwup, a reject, laughingstock, freak. That I wasn't going to be different, second best. No dork, sissy, a *cat*'olic from the cat faith.

I take out from my wallet the "No Blood" card and show it to my classmate. I'm not going to lie, not about Jehovah. "Regardless of circumstances, I do not agree to any form of blood transfusion (a transfusion of whole blood, plasma, red blood cells, white blood cells, platelets), even if in the judgment of a physician their use was necessary to save my health or life."—Signed by me and two witnesses. I further stipulate on the card that I relieve the doctors, hospitals, and their entire staff from liability for all such damages that could result from failing to provide blood.

Then she appears. Black eyes. It begins with them. Later it's a stroll, the best way to play hooky, a walk in the park, a tree, our tree for the coming time. I sit leaning against the trunk. She leans against me. Everything is blocked out by her hair. It smells nice. "Black-eyed," I say. "My colored-eyed," she replies, playing with my fingers. At our second meeting, at the dam near the park, I give her a letter so she'd know.

"Read."

"Now?"

I walk off toward the dam. I watch her with dread. She brushes away her hair and reads. At last she walks over, looks me in the eyes for a moment, takes me by the hand.

"Your religion makes no difference to me. It's cute that you were so worried."

After a few weeks of love, on November 20, 1995, she writes a letter to me: "You've been hiding something the whole time. You could use someone crazy, not a girlfriend. I'm not crazy."

We meet fifteen years later, when Black-Eyed comes back from Iceland, where she lives, to Poland for a brief visit. We sit in a restaurant in Szklarska Poręba. She orders dessert. Me, a coffee.

It's supposed to be different in high school. Just hide the shame and fear.

"What do you want from Santa Claus?"

"I don't celebrate it."

"Christmas?"

"Yeah."

"And presents?"

"We give each other presents all year long."

After this statement you should be jealous and not ask if that means that I get 365 presents a year. Yeah, no. Wrong. But no chance. Throughout the year. And not because we have to since it's Christmas, which is pagan anyway. Drop it. Pagan-schmagan. Be nice already.

It's different in high school. There's not a second black-eyed girl, but there are buddies.

The train from Szklarska Poręba leaves at 6:40. After an hour it's in Jelenia Góra. On the return you can always take the slow train. To sober up, for when you go for vodka and cigarettes instead of school. And to relish standing next to them in the hallway during break. Nothing going on. Simply standing next to each other. Buddies. I remember well. It's noon, on break. Laughing at somebody, me and my buddies. Laughing out loud. I hear that laughter. I'm with those who dish out nicknames. And later we talk.

"You have to lie on your back, on the bed for support."

"For support?"

"Yeah, like from behind, so you can hold your legs while you put them over your head."

"And you can reach it?"

"Yeah."

At night I strip naked, place my legs behind my head, using my hands to help. With my mouth I take hold of my penis. After a while my body goes numb. There are no thoughts. Not a single thought. And nothing hurts. A lightness. This is how it must be in paradise. I feel a bitter, sticky liquid on my tongue. I run to the bathroom ecstatic. I sensed that something very bad had happened. My ecstasy, pushed out by dread, quickly evaporates. I fall to my knees crying. I pray, bowing my head low, because that's how you talk to Jehovah. Saying I'm sorry is not enough, I know. He tells me this through shame and guilt. They make themselves comfortable inside me, welcomed with fear. I beg for forgiveness. I promise to be better. It takes me more than half an hour. Never again, I convince Jehovah. Never again.

I can't fall asleep. I pick up the book *Your Youth—Getting the Best out of It* from 1976. I open it to Chapter Five titled "Masturbation and Homosexuality." It says there how to assuage your curiosity. I read:

"Should you experiment with your sex organs? Is there anything wrong with rubbing them in some way until the excitement is climaxed? This practice is called masturbation" (35).

"God has provided marriage as the arrangement in which to satisfy sexual desires. But the person who practices masturbation is, in effect, trying to obtain that satisfaction without paying the price" (37).

"Masturbation weakens a healthy conscience and love for what is right..." (38).

"Weakly giving in to sexual desires by masturbation will certainly not give you strength when faced with a situation tempting you to commit fornication—or even homosexuality" (39).

"...you may find it helpful to sleep on your side rather than on your back or face down" (42).

"Proper hygiene calls for certain handling of the sex organs, and one might feel that this would be a temptation to misuse them. But because your motive is right—with the aim of *avoiding* sexual tension—you may well find that such care will instead help you to take a more healthful view toward these organs" (42-43).

I lie down on my side. I read on. You shouldn't eat a lot before bed. And sleep in a room with someone from the family in case temptations come at night. If this doesn't work, you can pray, talk with an elder, go for a walk, work out, or when Satan is tempting you, start reading the Bible out loud.

It's different in high school. Sometimes, every few weeks, classmates invite you for a drink. I'm going. I've been dying of shame and fear. Now I'm seeing what it's like to die from a sense of guilt.

It's different in high school. I walk around the kiosk in Jelenia Góra for three hours. I finally buy it. I split. Right where I was standing, the earth was torn asunder. It's a porno mag. I fight off thinking about Jehovah, that He's watching him all the time. That he's sad, angry. I know that. My Father in heaven is sad and angry, I know. It's already difficult. But the thought that He's watching it , watching my penis. I fight off the thought.

Every right pocket in my pants has a hole. The train ride takes an hour. It sometimes happens that there's an empty compartment. After all, I can't just pull out a Bible and start reading out loud every time.

Robert

Now I know. In the event of a tragedy we each have one emergency exit. We carry in ourselves this alternative scenario. Very few of those trampled by life make use of it. Unconsciously we choose from four options: kill yourself, kill somebody else, go crazy, or get sick. Our words betray us. At moments of tension or anger, being carefree or joking, or anytime we're otherwise intoxicated, we express our favorite concern: I'll kill myself, I'll kill you, maybe I'm going crazy, I'm definitely sick of this. We hear and wave our hand or indulgently smile, both we who hear it and they who say it.

All my life I thought that the emergency exit for him was to kill himself. Now it occurs to me that he had figured out a fifth solution: creating a new identity. Just like Piotr Odmieniec Włast who came from Maria Komornicka.[2] No new role, occupation, or new world that you can discover. Simply a new identity hung on the old structure of selfhood.

He thought about me when he was feeling guilty and alone. Only then. We met beside the notebook with the gray cover. That pretext was necessary for him to talk. We wrote with the same pen. Him one sentence, and then me one. I had to be his judge. I had to discipline and motivate him. It was him—of little faith, not yet a fanatic—who decided what we'd talk about and how. He was using me. Surrendering his thoughts, his every fear and doubt. He was counting on the pain, on the disgust, on me telling him to stop. So I wrote him to stop.

He couldn't handle a life in two worlds. The one with his classmates, their acceptance, camaraderie. And the one with the suit, Bible study, preaching. His inability to be completely with his peers and at the same time to be effortless in prayer before Jehovah aroused feelings of guilt, induced nightmares at night. He forced me into the role of God who is all-seeing. In one of our written

2 Maria Komornicka (1876-1949) was a Polish writer, poet, translator, and literary critic. At the age of 30, after burning all of her feminine clothing, she began to live her life as a man, Piotr Odmieniec Wlast. The middle name *Odmieniec* can be translated as *freak, weirdo, changeling, misfit*, and *creep.–Trans.*

conversations he started with the sentence, "I'm probably the flimsiest speck of dust, huh?" He couldn't have guessed then that the time would come when he'd have to die because of me.

Witnesses

On August 18, 1994, a special issue of *Awake!* entitled "Youths Who Put God First" came out. On its cover a photo of twenty-six children. All had put God first—they had refused a blood transfusion and had died.

Twelve-year-old Lena Martinez from California is suffering from leukemia. In the Valley Children's Hospital in Fresno, supported by her congregation and parents, she says, "I don't want any blood or any or its components. I prefer to die than to break a promise to fulfill the will of Jehovah God." And then she in fact dies.

Seventeen-year-old Crystal Moore goes to the clinic at Columbia University Presbyterian Medical Center in New York with ulcerative colitis. She refuses a transfusion. The case goes to the Supreme Court. Crystal says that if they try to give her a blood transfusion she'll "scream at the top of her lungs," that she considers forcing blood equally as abhorrent as rape. She dies.

Twelve-year-old Lisa Kosack from Toronto, who died at home in the arms of her parents, was asked by the court if she wanted to die. "Of course not. I don't think anyone wants that. But if I really die, I'm not scared of it since I expect to live forever in an earthly paradise."

When sick, a Jehovah's Witness goes to the hospital. Right behind him appears the Hospital Liaison Committee, usually made up of two or three elders. They present alternative treatments to a blood transfusion to the doctors, such as administering physiological saline, Ringer's solution, or dextran. They inform the hospital about the legal consequences of undertaking treatments against the wishes of the patient, who they support with prayer at the hospital bed.

For the prohibition against accepting blood, Jehovah's Witnesses rely on two passages from the Bible: "keep abstaining from things sacrificed to idols and from blood and from things strangled" (Acts 15:29) and "Only flesh with its soul—its blood—you must not eat." (Gen 9:4). Nowhere in the Bible can you find information about blood transfusions as such.

More and more often the decision to accept blood derivatives are seen as matters of conscience. However, the official position concerning transfusions remains unchanged. A question of conscience is a controversial behavior that does not result in expulsion from the congregation. If an unconscious Jehovah's Witness ends up at a hospital and donated blood is given to him, there are no harmful consequences. On the other hand, informed consent for a blood transfusion for their children or themselves means expulsion from the community.

The issue of *Awake!* describing the death of children who had put Jehovah first is no longer in official circulation. Just like many publications released a few years ago. On November 12, 2012, all congregations of Jehovah's Witnesses received a letter recommending the removal and destruction of their inventory of older literature. Bookcases in Kingdom Halls and in the homes of followers were emptied.

In the destroyed publications it was written, among other things, about attempts to determine the date of the end of the world despite the passage from the Bible that says, "Concerning that day or the hour nobody knows, neither the angels in heaven nor the Son, but the Father" (Mk 13:32). The last day was in 1975, when, according to Jehovah's Witnesses, six thousand years of human history on earth had passed, six thousand years from the time of Adam. In *The Watchtower* of August 1968 you could read: "A definitive end to the old scheme of things is approaching. Within at most a few years the final chapter of biblical prophecy about 'the last days' will be fulfilled."

At that time many followers in Poland as well as around the world prepared themselves for Armageddon. Some quit their jobs, others sold their property. Some put off their decision to have children, not knowing that they would have to wait decades for the next end of the world.

The year 1975 came and went. Just like 1914, 1918, 1920, and 1925, when the end of the world was also supposed to have come. The increase of followers in 1977 stood at minus one.

"In 1976, a year after the passing of that widely publicized date, a few members of the Governing Body began urging that some statement should be made acknowledging that the organization had been in error, had stimulated false expectations. Others said they did not think we should, that it would 'just give ammunition to opposers,'" wrote Raymond Franz in his *Crisis of Conscience* (209). For almost ten years he occupied the highest position in the organization of Jehovah's Witnesses: he belonged to the Governing Body. It is made up of only men, currently eight, who oversee all its activities. They interpret the Bible, develop the content of the printed literature, issue instructions for the congregations concerning the latest teachings, conduct meetings, oversee the construction of new assembly halls. Articles in *The Watchtower* and *Awake!* are not signed with a name. Just like the letter about destroying the literature, it comes from the Governing Body.

The shift in their position on the implementation of their teachings and the determination of the date of the end of the world is called "a new light," or it's said that "the light got brighter." God presents it to the men who make up the Governing Body and they communicate the news to the followers.

The light may be old, at which point it's false. The new light is true until it's replaced by something brighter.

This phrase was taken from the Proverbs of

Solomon: "But the good man walks along in the ever-brightening light of God's favor; the dawn gives way to morning splendor." (Prov 4:18 TLB). In the New World Translation prepared by the Jehovah's Witnesses the verse reads, "But the path of the righteous ones is like the bright light that is getting lighter and lighter until the day is firmly established." The Warsaw Bible speaks about "the full light of day," and the Gdańsk Bible about "the perfect day." A new day full of light in the strictest sense is noon. Figuratively, it could mean a moment of understanding, enlightenment, awakening, an experience of paradise, or something entirely different that maybe only Solomon knew.

Jehovah's Witnesses have a knack for adjusting to the decreed teachings of Bible passages; sometimes, as in this case, it's turned into metaphor.

Luke

"Today I'm going to the center. I don't care. I'll probably not kill myself just yet. I've decided to ignore everyone and everything," I write in my journal on July 8, 1996.

On July 29 I add: "Everything's okay. It was super. I met Grześ. Everything's changed. I'm going to a second center. I see a lot of things completely differently."

The entry on August 27 begins: "Frenzy—I returned from the second center and immediately went to a third. I want to become a pioneer, starting in September, for as long as I have enough energy."

I go to the first center together with my brother, at my parents' suggestion. Dad buys each of us a tent. Plawidla, near Zytno. Immediately after arriving we pitch our tents next to a large military site that had been converted into a kitchen and a place for evening meetings. Grzeš and Mariusz lead a group of over twenty people. Rise-and-shine is around seven. The two people who are on duty change every day. They keep an eye on the tents and prepare meals for everyone. In the meantime, the rest of us head out to preach in the surrounding villages. The young and inexperienced, like me, go with the older pioneers. Always in pairs. Over the next two weeks everyone's goal is to spend sixty hours in service to Jehovah. We need to drum up as many interested people as we can and take notes on them to pass along to the brothers from the local congregation. I especially like returning to camp. I don't have to watch what I say. We already speak the same language. We're family. I make friends. One evening I confide in Grzeš my sins in high school. I repent and cry. Then I talk a long time with Jehovah. I fall asleep during my prayers, which I return to over the next few days. In the end, God forgives me.

At the second center, near Rzeszów, there's Diana, a friend and distant cousin. We spend every free moment with each other. We go out together to preach and don't return until more than ten hours later. It's a record for our center. Over the next few years we'll call ourselves friends and take care of each other. We'll sign up to take guitar lessons together. We'll go to Radom for a week to preach. I'll visit her in Wojcieszyce, where she lives. Sometimes we sit on the window ledge in her room to spit on the old pear tree and talk for hours. I'll take my last walk with her before leaving for college. We'll create our own dictionary. We call euphoria, joy, high spirits "Jamaica." We call sadness, depression, bad thoughts about death, which we share in common, "Japan."

I'll miss her for many years. Till the very end. She stopped replying to my letters. She didn't want to meet with me to say goodbye even for a few minutes. She stayed with Jehovah, sacrificing our friendship to Him. The choice is always obvious.

The second center ends. I'm going to Zakopane with a few pioneers. I don't ask my parents for permission. I send them a card so they won't worry. It's not until we're in the mountains that I confess to my brothers that I didn't get permission. At their disappointed looks I say that, after all, I wasn't forbidden either. I don't remember ever having been happier. We have three days until heading to the next pioneer center. We hike Eagle's Path. We sleep in stone huts. Every morning we read the Bible, pray, eat a meal, and then wander around. We sing songs, talk. Me and Grześ, about four years older than me, a regular pioneer. A man like I'd like to be. A true servant of Jehovah.

I'm at the third center for only a few days when I have to go back home. Clean clothes ran out faster than money. I reminisce about Eagle's Path.

We went backpacking for three days. We looked at the mountains. We were so small before God. The return by train. I lay my head on Grzeš' shoulder, pretending to be asleep. For a few hours with my eyes closed, I feel special because of the friendship I found thanks to Jehovah.

"The worldly make me want to puke. I look at learning differently, and generally I see the meaning of life. Besides, I have some goals that I have to sort out," I write in my journal on September 3, 1996, in my second year of high school.

In September I submit an application to serve as an auxiliary pioneer. Getting to Jelenia Góra and back takes two hours, school, then you have to do your homework. Meetings Tuesday, Friday, and Sunday. To that, add field service and personal study, and still there's fruit to bear: sixty hours of preaching a month. On average two hours a day. I don't always have time for it. I make up for it on Saturdays and Sundays, when I preach for six hours or more.

The time of letters begins. Sometimes it happens that five arrive in a day, from all over Poland. From male and female cousins, from brothers and sisters, from Grzeš and Diana. We relate our reality to one another. We share our favorite verses.

"I'm very glad that as a tool in God's hands I could help you. Jehovah knows well what hurt you—that's why He chose the best medicine. In life I wouldn't lift a finger for our friendship if I wasn't entirely convinced that it'd yield a real, sincere connection with Jehovah. If someone asks for one reason that makes it worth serving Jehovah, for me, one verse is enough: Revelation 4:11. Don't shrug off the displays of kindness from your parents or from Jehovah. Jehovah gave many gifts to young servants and observes who uses them well. Take care."–Grześ writes on September 10, 1996.

I take care of myself. I take to heart the often-repeated recommendation at meetings to end contact with your classmates at the last school bell. I feel bad for Krzysiek, Ula, Jola, and Irmina. We like each other. My religion doesn't bother them, but I shouldn't be friends with them. Satan is crafty. I don't have time to regret it, so I feel bad for only a moment. I apply to serve as an auxiliary pioneer again in October. And again in November.

"I've been a pioneer for five months already. The day before yesterday I came back from Radomsko. I miss preaching longer hours. I got to know Przemek better. I want to go there again for a week. I'm very happy because I'm finally living the truth. I love God, my parents, my brother, and people."–I jot down November 18, 1996. Przemek had gone from Jelenia Góra to preach where there's a greater need. He lives at the Kingdom Hall. He organizes weeklong (and longer) visits to him for young pioneers. I am a frequent visitor and an admirer. I am in love with his solitary devotion to Jehovah.

"Today I begin the seventeenth year of my life. It doesn't matter anyway. I wanted to take Prozac, but I was scared. I'm still waffling. I know it's stupid.

MOP is killing me. My life could go ahead and end today."–I write on December 1, my birthday. MOP is short for "masturbation and onanism prevention." In my earlier diaries I notated every sin with a made-up abbreviation.

The day before at our meeting we analyzed Jesus' words: "If, then, your hand or your foot is making you stumble, cut it off and throw it away from you; it is finer for you to enter into life maimed or lame than to be thrown with two hands or two feet into the everlasting fire. Also, if your eye is making you stumble, tear it out and throw it away from you; it is finer for you to enter one-eyed into life than to be thrown with two eyes into the fiery Gehenna" (Mt 18:8-9).

I know that the hand, foot, and eye are symbols of what interferes with you serving, of what sidetracks, tempts, pulls you from the truth. I also know that sometimes the Bible is like a double-edged sword, saying explicitly what needs to be done. "Cut off and throw it away from you." I mull over these words. I'm afraid of complications. How will I urinate?

Every few weeks, sometimes even days, I give in. Then I can't pray to Jehovah. I lose His blessing. I upset my Father in heaven. In addition, I force Him to watch me do it. My disgust with myself is often unbearable. It invites thoughts of death. In my journal I quote the words of Solomon: "I congratulated the dead who had already died" (Eccl 4:2).

I don't have the courage. The place for it is filled

with shame. I don't dare talk with a congregation elder or with Grzeš, Przemek, or Diana. Before I find the courage to return to Jehovah, sometimes several hours go by. Or even days. The matter is simpler in that God already knows, more difficult in that it's God we're talking about. Such a prayer takes a long time. It's always for a long time. It begins with an apology until I myself can hardly believe it. My chin pressed to my chest.

I'm sorry, very sorry, Jehovah. I'm not trying hard enough, I know. I ask Your forgiveness, Jehovah. You know what I did. I'm sorry. I don't preach enough. I don't pray enough. I don't read the Bible every morning. I don't really study the literature very carefully. I give in. I know it's not enough from me. I don't believe strong enough because if I had faith as a grain of mustard seed I'd move mountains, I know. Or less than a seed. Maybe like half. I'd preach more, work more in the congregation. And I wouldn't do it anymore. Never again. And since I give in to myself, for pleasure, for brief pleasure, it means I'm weak. But You are strong and hand out mercy when someone asks You. I'm not asking right. Too little. And my faith, too small. But the size of a mustard seed would be enough. Mine's going to be bigger. I'm sorry, God, beloved Dad, Father in heaven, Jehovah. I'm sorry. Change—. Change me, please. I don't want to be disgusting in Your eyes. Change me, please.

I made the decision on the way to school to cut off my penis.

Witnesses

Yahweh [Jahwe], Jehovah [Jehowa] is the Polonized tetragrammaton YHWH [JHWH] that appears almost seven thousand times in the Hebrew Scriptures. Moses, setting off for the Israelites, plans to tell them that God has sent him. "'Suppose I am now come to the sons of Israel and I do say to them, "The God of your forefathers has sent me to you," and they do say to me, "What is his name?" What shall I say to them?' At this God said to Moses: "I SHALL PROVE TO BE WHAT I SHALL PROVE TO BE." And he added: "This is what you are to say to the sons of Israel, 'I SHALL PROVE TO BE has sent me to you'" (Ex 3:13-14).

Perhaps in this way God was saying that knowing Him isn't possible. However, it generally turns out well for religious people. They believe in a personal God who loves and gets angry, rejoices and grieves, shows mercy but also remembers your sins, even those of our fathers' fathers'. They believe in a jealous God who should be feared.

Jehovah sent a flood to destroy almost all the people and animals. He also sent His son to die in agony and to save the world. Before long, Jehovah will send fire from heaven to destroy the wicked during Armageddon. The millions killed will become "as manure on the surface of the ground" (Jer 25:33). It's all out of love. (Luke thought about this manure when they laughed at him when he was preaching. About the stench of decaying bodies covering almost the entire earth. Sometimes he and his brothers and sisters wondered how fast they'd be able to bury them all. Of course, if they survive.)

Those who had rejected the truth would die. That's why Witnesses try to knock on every door: to reach all the people who live behind them.

An eternal paradise will reign on earth. No exhaust fumes, pollution, violence, war, sickness, or death. There will be plenty of healthy food, and "the wolf and the lamb themselves will feed as one, and the lion will eat straw just like the bull; and as for the serpent, his food will be dust" (Isa 65:25). Such a paradise. At that time the just and the unjust will be resurrected. The latter for judgment, the rest to life everlasting.

Paradise on earth awaits all of Jehovah's faithful servants except for 144,000 who will live in heaven with Jesus Christ. In 1914 He began putting things in order. He cast Satan and his demons from heaven while those on earth unleashed the First World War. Before long, order will come to pass on earth as well.

In the book *You Can Live Forever in Paradise on Earth* from 1982 it's written: "Some of the generation living in 1914 will see the end of the system of things and survive it" (154). With growing hope, many followers worked out how old the members of that generation would have to be. Time went by. People from the generation born before 1914 dwindled. The still living were over eighty, ninety years old. Armageddon didn't come. Instead, the light got brighter, and it turned out that it was about a different generation.

On the fourteenth day of the month of Nisan, the first month of the Jewish religious calendar (late March or early April) Jehovah's Witnesses celebrate their only holiday—the Memorial of Jesus Christ's Death. During the hour-long lecture, an elder reflects on the Lord's Evening Meal, reads the Bible, and prays. Followers pass unleavened bread on a plate and red wine in a glass from hand to hand. Symbols of the body and blood of Jesus. "Emblems" in the language of the followers. Only those going to heaven can consume them. Deciding whether you are one of the anointed is based on a feeling, though it is Jehovah Himself who anoints.

In 2014 the Memorial was attended by over nineteen million people, but only 14,121 consumed the emblems, as mentioned in the *Yearbook of Jehovah's Witnesses*. These are the latest figures on the 144,000 anointed to reign in heaven.

(In the congregation in Szklarska Poreba, all the brothers and sisters waited for life everlasting in paradise on earth. There wasn't anyone anointed to heaven. When I asked Luke what would happen if he ate a piece of the bread, he looked at me very seriously and confessed that he'd then be eating his own death.)

Robert

As a rule, he waited for a better life, for paradise. Or he reminisced. He couldn't deal with transience. He collected the past in letters, diaries, in thousands of saved notes jotted down. He recorded conversations with friends on a tape recorder. He took lots of pictures. He couldn't believe in happiness when it came. At those times he'd pull out a camera or a notepad and pen in order to hang on to what it was.

Jehovah's Witnesses live for the future, so they can't do anything that might bring them fame. They shouldn't paint, sculpt, compose or—like him—write. He left that to me, even though he dreamed of writing. It was then that he felt free.

January 1, 1997, he logged in his diary: "I lose myself. I want to, but I don't have the strength. Why?" His feelings of guilt combined with his longing for death were interwoven with the hope of surviving Armageddon that paved the way for his perpetually undertaken struggle for moral purity. He despised himself for masturbating.

Luke

I take a knife from the kitchen. I go upstairs to the second story. I enter the bathroom, turn on the light. I drop my pants to the floor, pull down my underwear. I apply the knife to the base of my penis. Wait. I'm scared of the pain, that I'll bleed to death. I gently drag it across the skin. It stings. It leaves a red line on the flesh. I won't do it. I'm too weak even for that.

I'm too weak even for that, I think. I go to my own room, full of hate and helplessness regarding a body I didn't choose, into my head, my wicked, sinful head I didn't choose. I lie in bed and think about the words: "Keep on asking, and it will be given you; keep on seeking, and you will find; keep on knocking, and it will be opened to you" (Lk 11:9). I'm beginning to understand. It'll be given to me. I'll find. It'll be opened to me. It suddenly becomes clear. I have to ask more. To seek differently. To knock louder. The thorn will then disappear.

February 1, 1997, I become the first regular pioneer in town. From now on I'll allocate ninety hours every month for preaching. My parents ask if I'd thought through my decision since with school, the commute, and meetings I won't have time for anything.

"Who told me when I was little that we must first seek the Kingdom of God and God's justice and it'll be given to us? Does the Bible lie?"

"That's not what..."

"If it doesn't lie, then all the rest will be given to me, right?"

"Please, think about it."

"First the Kingdom!"

I laugh out loud. I dance. Because I already know. And my knowledge is my faith. It's fairly straightforward: love Jehovah more than the world, more than yourself, far more than school. My happiness is my faith.

My parents let me make up my own mind. I'm

happy. I join the ranks of men, the company of those who I look up to at meetings and conventions. I wanted to be like them. I'm especially happy because I have hope that Jehovah will now help me. If I spend a thousand hours in one year preaching I'll be invited to the special pioneer training course, which nobody out of the several dozen people in my family has ever been to.

March 1, 1997, in my sophomore year, I ditch the technical high school with the applied microeconomics tract in Jelenia Góra and transfer to the advanced economics high school.[3]

I arrived in the middle of my Polish class to say goodbye. I don't know how to explain to them. I want to leave quickly, to run away, to not feel the regret, the closeness, the attachments, the loss. To not feel anything.

March 9, 1997, I receive a letter from Jola, a friend from class: "I was disappointed. You didn't explain to me the reason why you left school. The principal was talking about your situation. From that, I found out you changed schools because of your religion. I don't know how to adequately gauge this, but apparently you want to be some kind of preacher of the Word of God. Without you, classes are boring and unappealing. I miss being stupid with you, our conversations, and even your

3 The two most common types of Polish high schools are the liceum (which I translate as "high school") and the technikum (or *liceum techniczne*). The liceum prepares students for higher education. Graduates of a technikum, where students learn technical and vocational skills, usually enter the workforce.—*Trans.*

annoying teasing and writing all over my notebook. (Your signature's everywhere I look, which only reminds me of the times we spent together). Know that if you come back I'll give up my spot in Room 213 permanently so you'll be able to copy with no problem. Jola."

I'm not going back. Now I have classes every two weeks, on Saturday and Sunday. And plenty of time for preaching. I'm one of the youngest in class. Most are around thirty years old. In my first class the lecturer asks how many F's I had at my previous school. None. D's? None. She looks at me for a moment. Everyone's looking. When someone transfers from daily school to weekends, he usually does it because of grades. C's? None. I had the third highest average at my previous school. I don't fit in here either. It doesn't matter. I didn't come to make friends, but it's proof of a life in the truth, not fitting in. I have to get credit for seven subjects in two month's time, including office technology, typing, and Russian, even though I don't know Cyrillic. I previously had studied German and English.

I set aside all my free time for preaching.

My territory is Lower Szklarska Poreba. There's still Central and Upper as well. For my service I arrange to meet with every willing person from the congregation. With Włodek, who, after a stroke, walks with crutches. With Maja (who's about Włodek's age), who, after several months and lots of persuasion, will also become a pioneer.

With my own mom, who, after several hours of preaching, I sometimes sit with downtown eating pizza. When I can't find a partner to preach with, I write letters to acquaintances and to strangers. I give my testimony in them. I begin studying the Bible with Asia, a friend from the congregation, who I've played with at home since childhood. Once she even delivered my baby. I had given birth to a teddy bear. Later we'd go on long walks, and I was fascinated hearing about her marriage. Now once a week, with the Bible and compassion, her mother and I bow our heads in prayer for Asia, who's unwilling to get baptized.

I urge everyone to enter pioneer service. I begin preaching to my friends and family. If my parents had their hearts right, they also would've become pioneers. I tell them this again and again.

On occasion I preach outside my own territory, in Central Szklarska Poręba, in the apartment block where classmates from my old grade school live. I see the name of my Polish teacher on a door I have to knock on. The candies are going back into a brown paper bag. Her glare when I refused to learn that ancient Polish hymn the "Mother of God." I'm sitting on the school bench all over again. This time I'm wearing a suit and have a Bible in hand. I came to teach my teacher. I came to convert her. My body is ready to walk down the stairs and go to the next door. Then I remember about Peter, who denied Jesus three times. He was caught and interrogated at the home of Caiaphas. Peter was sorry and wept. I ring the doorbell. I hear footsteps. Someone peeks through the peephole. And nothing, silence. I wait a moment, for as long as it takes to come out, and I leave. I never tell anyone that I was afraid, that I was ashamed of who I was, that I was a coward just like Peter.

I glue dried flowers on a piece of white paper. In the center I put a quote written in pencil: "holding faith and a good conscience, which some have thrust aside and have experienced shipwreck concerning their faith" (1 Tim 1:19). I put the picture in a wooden frame and hang it in my room. It's supposed to remind me.

"Only one MOP in November. A week ago some murderer killed a woman in Lower Szklarska. I had been at her place earlier to preach. I yearn for Armageddon."–I write in my diary on November 30, 1997.

More and more often it happens that I conduct meetings. I want to be a ministerial servant. Then an elder of the congregation. And after finishing school, go to Russia as a missionary. Because there's a need there. Or go to the Bethel Home. Only I'm still too young, and they won't take me with my thorn. It's nothing. I'll wait. Jehovah will help.

Witnesses

Bethel is a biblical city, identified with the modern Beitin, located not far from Jerusalem. In a literal translation from Hebrew, Bethel means "house of God."

The Jehovah's Witnesses' Headquarters, located since 1909 in the New York borough of Brooklyn, is called Bethel. Members of the Governing Body live and work there. They oversee ninety branch offices, also called Bethel, scattered all over the world. In 2014 there were 24,711 volunteers who lived and worked there, publishing the *Yearbook of Jehovah's Witnesses*. The Polish Bethel Home has its headquarters in Nadarzyn near Warsaw, at ul. Warszawska 14.

There are various myths that circulate on the subject of money that followers receive from Brooklyn. A lot of people start going to meetings and studying with Witnesses hoping for material benefits. In reality, the organization is sustained by voluntary donations. Boxes, into which you can throw your money, can be found in every Kingdom Hall and at every large assembly.

Congregation elders, ministerial servants, pioneers, and all the men who hold a position in the organization can marry, have children. Although they devote their time in service to Jehovah, they should support themselves and their family. Only missionaries, Bethel Home workers, and traveling brothers, who have paid health insurance premiums and retirement, reimbursed travel expenses, as well as a small monthly salary, are exempt from this requirement.

In 2014 more than $224 million was allocated for this purpose.

A traveling brother oversees the activity of several congregations located near one another. He visits them—often with his wife—once every six months. On each visit he stays for a week. The followers provide him with accommodations and full board. Sometimes they hand over the money from voluntary contributions to him in an envelope. In 2014, followers' contributions in the amount of one złoty a month from every preacher was established. Every month a collected quota—about 123,000 złoty—has to be spent on cars for the traveling brothers.

Sometimes a resolution concerning the building of a new Kingdom Hall is announced. Preachers pledge how much they'll allocate each month toward that goal on a special form.

Unmarried Jehovah's Witnesses sometimes leave a legacy of all their possessions to the organization. Though it is recommended that Jehovah be given at least ten percent (Mal 3:10) of your time and material resources, each makes a decision on this matter individually and typically anonymously. Most of the money goes to the Bethel Home in Brooklyn.

In recent years the organization's office buildings are gradually being sold off, like the thirty-storied skyscraper printshop that was a place of employment and housing for about a thousand people. "The five properties, with combined asking prices of $18.8 million, are going on the market this weekend," wrote Sarah Kershaw in her article "Big Deal: Jehovah's Witnesses List Prime Properties" in *The New York Times* on September 16, 2011. Three years later the newspaper reported that over the last ten years the Witnesses had sold more than thirty buildings in Brooklyn, including the printshop, historic tenements, and the famous Hotel Bossert, for $81 million.

In July 2009 the organization bought a property with an area of 252 acres in Warwick, New York. By 2017 the headquarters will be moved there, and other buildings will occupy more than forty-four acres of the area surrounded by forests and wetlands.

Robert

"I'm sick of this dialog. You can be exposed to the winds, and even though you may sway, your feet are still firmly planted,"–he wrote to me March 21, 1997, in the notebook with the gray cover. It was one of our last joint entries.

There are such evenings when he and I sit in his room. It's dark. He's thinking about death. Talking about death. He'll want me to write something, so I write. We meet only when he's suffering. I gradually disappear from his life. His new friendships now absorb him—Diana, Ewelina, Grześ, as well as the others from the congregations scattered around Jelenia Góra. To this you can add in the centers, the meetings with pioneers, trips to Radomsko, reading the Bible, and writing letters.

Luke

I'm standing with my feet wide apart. My body is bent over so that I'm looking between my legs, and I'm walking backwards. "Run away, wolf," I say, "run away!" Then the mailman shows up. "To the Extraordinary Lost Boy who I managed to fall in love with in only four days. Your friend, Peter Pan." The inscription was written with a pen. I recognize the handwriting. I read it once. Then again and again. I shout and dance around my room. Peter Pan left less than a week ago and he did what he promised. He sent me a copy of *The Adventures of Peter Pan*. And in it a little magic dust from Tinker Bell, his girlfriend, a fairy.

"Second street to the right and then straight on till morning"—that's where we'll meet. Kids, lost boys who fell out of their prams when the nurse was looking the other way. "If they are not claimed in seven days they are sent far away to the Neverland." They're a little homesick, but only a little, because they quickly get to know their captain, Peter Pan, and, together with him, find adventures. But it's not hide-and-seek or hopscotch or even a cheap vacation package to Egypt. Real adventures. Pirates, mermaids—these things. I pick the name Sleepy Head for myself.

I soon learn that "winking is the star language," that swallows build their nests under thatched roofs because they want "to listen to the stories," and the only reason birds fly and we do not is that they have faith. And—what is quite brutal—when a child says he doesn't believe in fairies, one of them drops dead. I learned what's most important in Neverland: how to scare off wolves. You have to stand with your legs straight, slightly bowed, with your back to the wolf. Then you should bend over so you can look the wolf in the eyes between your legs. Then you should walk backwards in its direction. It works. We confirmed it several times at Marooners' Rock where Hook hunted for Tinker Bell.

And now come the letters.

"Oh, Sleepy Head! Must I write you how much I love you and how happy I am with every adventure that we will surely experience together? The thought that eternal life could turn out to be an endless adventure is the sustenance of happiness for me. All adults are pirates. Don't trust them. I'll be seeing you in my dreams. Your friend."–May 7, 1997.

"I'm worried about you on account of those exams and nonstop assignments. Fortunately, in Neverland you can forget about it if but for a moment. As for Russian ... the fairy Svetlana, who comes from the Asian Neverland, has decided (at Tinker Bell's urging) that she'll help you. I'm telling you, there's no problem at all. Svetlana is so small that she can easily be hidden in your ear. As a result, she can whisper the answers. But watch out! When *I love you* is said, fairies grow. See how large my Tinker Bell has grown. When this cruel moment of despair seizes you, remember that you can always count on me. Let's run away somewhere together where nobody will ever look for us. I love you. Your older brother."–May 25, 1997.

"I understand the inhabitants of my Neverland. That thanks to my imagination, this island is alive. And although my entire childhood has passed (I've turned twenty years old), I'm still a boy in a green outfit."–August 17, 1997.

"I love your letters. Only thanks to Jehovah's love do I manage to get through each exam crammed with problems. You know, Sleepy Head, it's not true that it's easy for me to show affection."–October 20, 1997.

"You know what Neverland really is? A longing for paradise. For a world free from violence, deceit, and lies. The theme of death is often winding through your letters and poems. If you want to talk about it, no problem. But don't let those destructive thoughts destroy your spiritual mind. I'm having problems understanding Robert. Write specifically about what's going on with this Robert."–November 19, 1997.

"It's bad. Adulthood has infiltrated the consciousness of the inhabitants of Neverland. I'm not stupid. I don't eat make-believe food when I'm hungry. Grześ often wonders how you can maintain the balance between reality and playing in Neverland. I'd very much like it if we could go crazy someday. Like for real. Painting our faces, pinning feathers to a war bonnet, planning a party with fairies, and a campfire with Indians. Don't forget about me. I believe in you. I hope that you also believe in me. I love you. Your friend and brother."–May 19, 1998.

I make up for the deficiencies from the past three semesters until the end of June. For the Russian exam I take Svetlana with me. But I'm so stressed out and Svetlana is so tired from her journey from Asia that during the exam we don't even speak to one another. Later, she spreads the news to everyone in Neverland that she had helped me a lot.

After a few weeks of exchanging letters and taking vows of loyalty to Neverland, my friend Diana joins in. One night we paint our faces, pin feathers to our war bonnets, and arrange a party. Everything exactly like Peter Pan wanted. Later, even more brothers and sisters join us. We organize secret meetings in Jelenia Góra and Szklarska Poreba. Peter Pan is also a pioneer, so when we meet in a larger cluster of brothers at assemblies, we exchange only furtive glances. We create our own honor code. Peter Pan decides who we'll accept.

When my cousin learns about Neverland, he is shocked and speaks to the elders about us. They question Peter Pan. They warn that playing eats up valuable time that should belong to Jehovah. They warn about the cult of fiction. The demons of Satan take on various forms, and everything that distracts from the worship of Jehovah comes from them. Neverland disappears forever.

"But we're pioneers. Thanks to Neverland I love Jehovah even more," I explain.

"There are worse things," explains Peter Pan.

Robert

To Peter, I was Hook. A danger. He worried that I was distracting him from Jehovah. And I envied them these magical meetings, letters, confessions. Peter Pan was the first man who showed him how it was possible to articulate love in a friendship.

Witnesses

Dinah, the daughter of Jacob, the father of the twelve sons from whose names we get the names of the twelve tribes of Israel, is going to Canaan "to see the daughters of the land" (Gen 34:1). She is raped by Prince Shechem, who later wants to marry her. Jacob's sons agree to the marriage if Shechem and all the men in the city submit to getting circumcised. On the third day after the procedure Dinah's brothers, Jehovah's servants, plunder the city. The women and children are carried off into captivity, and they murder the prince and Canaanites.

Dinah was raped because she had befriended the worldly. She caused problems for her own brothers and brought death upon the Canaanites. This story is even told to small children of Jehovah's Witnesses. It's a warning against what contact with the world and indecent behavior leads to. And whoever offends his brothers deserves a millstone hung around his neck and pitched into the sea (Mk

9:42). Elders don't practice this biblical technique. Only a visit and a reproof, sometimes in public, await the person who offends his fellow believers.

During a meeting a woman might offend with a skirt revealing her knees, or a man without a suit and tie.

It's offensive to use profanity, to make inappropriate jokes.

It's offensive to spend time with a person of the opposite sex without supervision. In the Bethel Home, when a sister visits her brother in his room, the door to the hallway must remain open.

It's offensive to organize sports or any other pastime requiring spending time with the worldly.

Most homosexuals went down the wrong path "by spending time thinking about it and by associating with others who were that way"—I read in the book *Your Youth—Getting the Best Out of It* (121). That's why it's offensive to go to the movies to see films showing immorality, especially violence and sex. (During the pioneer center in Radomsko, Luke and his brothers went to the movies to see the comedy *High School High*. They left in the middle of the film and demanded their money back.)

On June 18, 2013, the Governing Body sent a letter to the congregation elders prohibiting brothers and sisters getting together in a larger group even if its aim was preparing for meetings: "The creation of private groups for joint Bible study is not recommended by the organization, and we ask for the cessation of this practice," since "a worrying trend associated with organizing such meetings is the desire to have fun afterwards. Unfortunately, such meetings often ended with the consumption of alcohol and dancing."

Alcohol is allowed, but in limited amounts. Drunkenness is a sin just like taking drugs or smoking cigarettes, for which you can be disfellowshipped from the organization. (Luke had never seen his parents drunk.)

To offend means to cause anxiety, fear, apprehension. This may produce doubts, fiendish thoughts. The compensation for severing ties with the world and its precepts is your sense of security. No stranded Jehovah's Witness will go hungry, and he'll always have a place to live.

When in November 2013 a typhoon destroyed the homes of followers in the Philippines, fundraisers were organized, temporary accommodations were prepared, and groups of young people from all over the world helped in the reconstruction of homes. The same was true a few years earlier in Brazil, when floods and landslides killed hundreds of people. Witnesses provided the needy forty-two tons of food, twenty thousand bottles of water, ten tons of clothes, five tons of cleaning products. In 2012 Hurricane Sandy destroyed twelve Kingdom Halls and hundreds of followers' residences on the eastern seaboard of the United States. They all received material and spiritual assistance from their brothers and sisters. This is what happens during every natural disaster. And when lonely or elderly Jehovah's Witnesses need help.

Luke

Fully aware of my decision—of sound body and mind—in case of unforeseen circumstances that may result in my death, I put in writing:

–my guitar as a token of friendship to my cousin Blazej,

–the contents of my black briefcase (letters, diaries, and magnetic stripe cards) to my dear friend Ewelina,

–my Peter Pan book to my friend Diana,

–my parrots Birdie and Judy to my friend Peter Pan (as well as my stuffed cow and happy thoughts),

–my Teddy bear Dreptusia to the best mom in the world,

–my picture of the boy and girl in the forest to the best brother,

–the picture with the flowers and the quote from 1 Timothy 1:18-19 to my beloved dad.

PS Forgive me the letter.

I hide my will dated December 12, 1997, prepared in Szklarska Poreba, at the back of my diary between pages glued together with the words, "Open only after my death." To my will I append permission to donate my organs and a letter:

To You!

I love all of you. It was seven friendships. Each of you have taught me something, have given a lot. And each of you, I believe, I'll see in that better world. I beg you, do everything to survive Armageddon. I hope that I will be resurrected. There is nothing better, more valuable, or that provides greater happiness than the path of Jehovah—please tread down it! It's already not far off. Already it'll be Armageddon tomorrow. See you soon. Your dear friend, son, brother, and cousin—Luke Zamilski.

Armageddon is a story about death. As are my thoughts. The last day of December I have a tradition of asking myself if next year will be the last. I always answer yes. Armageddon will come in the new year.

In February it will have been twelve months since I became a regular pioneer. I've worked 1,001 hours per thousand required. Now I'm also leaving for pioneer centers in the winter, over break. Sometimes I arrange to preach in the villages surrounding Jelenia Góra. Or I go to Radomsko, where there's a lot of territory. "In the Kingdom, if I find myself there, I'll ask Abel if his parents, Adam and Eve, had navels. Tomek asked me about it during study. He's been addicted to drugs and cigarettes for eight years. Now with the Bible's help he's trying to quit."–I write in my diary March 23, 1998.

Two Witnesses usually conduct Bible study at the home of someone interested. Meetings are held once or twice a week. They last an hour or more. Study begins with a prayer.

I bow my head and close my eyes. I ask for Jehovah's help and blessings for Tomek. We open the book *Knowledge That Leads to Everlasting Life* from 1995. For every section there's a question and verse from the Bible to read. There's tea on the table, sometimes cake. I like to study with Tomek. He talks a lot about his adventures. From him I learn about the game stone table. Several people sit at a table. Best if it's round. One person goes under the table and services the others.

"Services?" I ask.

"You know, orally."

"That's indecent," I comment, worked up.

Tomek chuckles and tells me to listen.

"And all the people at the table are looking at each other. Their faces must be like stone. Whoever lets on that he's being serviced or that he came goes under the table."

End of story, the end of study. Prayer—a bit longer prayer. And I'm off to someone I just met who's interested, who I want to persuade to study.

I'm leaving for the pioneer center in Nozynko with Diana. Preaching in the village, we talk for more than half an hour with a man who wants us to prove to him that a turtle is not God.

"But what kind of turtle," Diana wonders.

"The kind that lives in the ocean."

The man is serious. He raises questions, listens to our answers. He doesn't want to persuade us to believe in the turtle God. He wants *us* to convince *him* that a turtle doesn't feel, doesn't think. That a turtle isn't God. I pull out my Bible, and with it successive arguments. Ever more scripture. The man asks even more questions. Diana and I can't manage to get through to him. Instead he stirs up something in us that we don't know. We leave. Along the way we pray. We know that Satan had to have been guiding him. We hand over his address to more experienced elders. We'll not be going back there ourselves on account of Satan and the demons living with this man.

We get together in the evenings, after preaching and meetings. I wait until the camp gets dark. I sneak into David's tent. He lives with a guy also named Luke. We light a candle, talk in whispers. A few hours earlier we had bought some cans of beer. We pull out a stopwatch. We organize races—the first to finish drinking one. I win with a time of twenty-four seconds, next is Luke with forty-one seconds, and David with forty-five seconds. The next night Diana, Ewelina, and Ania come to the tent. They bring a yellow sixteen-ounce mug so it'll be easier to drink. First place is Luke—twelve seconds, then me—thirteen, David—twenty, Ania—twenty-two seconds, Diana—twenty-three, and Ewelina—twenty-four.

We cover our mouths with our hands when we start laughing. We advise Ewelina to swallow more air, but that doesn't help. For several minutes it takes its toll. She has a stomachache. Finally, she lets out a sound that goes on and on and on. Our hands pressed even harder over our mouths, we can't stop laughing, which carries on all night. The brothers in their tents with thick walls like cotton must have heard us.

The next day a reprimand awaits us. I'm the only regular pioneer in the group. I should've been a role model. I behaved shamefully. In a few days I'm supposed to go to my dream pioneer training course that I had to put in a thousand hours for. Now maybe I'm not going anywhere. I plead and apologize.

In the evening the center directors let me off the hook. It ends with a public reproof.

We get together the next night. We talk several hours, sans candle and in whispers, about death. Every one of us thinks about it. Sometimes. I shouldn't be talking. As a pioneer I shouldn't talk longingly about death. But it's so dark, and we're so close.

We light a lighter. Somebody presses it to my back. Then to their own hands. It leaves scars.

"My payoff from the center is 60½ hours. I was the only one who exceeded sixty hours. Little joy since I wanted to have a hundred this month."–I note July 30, 1998, on the road to Berlin for an international convention, where more than forty thousand followers from all over the world will attend.

Robert

Today on Facebook I sent a friend request to Diana.

I wrote that I had read her letters to Luke, that I'd gladly meet for a coffee and talk. She accepted my invitation. I wanted to see in her photos how she looked after all these years. After a day she unfriended me. It wasn't easy for her, this contact. "Of all the people who drifted away, the one I miss most is Luke. I continually delude myself that maybe someday he'll come back. Greetings, I wish you happiness."–She wrote November 11, 2014, adding that we won't be meeting, and for me to forgive her. "I'd gladly have a coffee with Luke. It's too much for me to share with Robert."

Luke

Mieroszów near Walbrzych. Twenty-four regular pioneers from Lower Silesia. Together with Tomek, a disabled pioneer from Karpacz. We get a room with a family of three.

Two circuit overseers, two traveling brothers, conduct the ten-day Pioneer Service School. Local sisters cook meals for us. Everyone gets a secret book with a blue cover titled *Shining as Illuminators in the World*. We can't share it with family members or congregation elders. Anyone. From this book (revised in 2004) come all the quotations in this section. Before us is a training program that will take twenty-three hours, including four hours of hands-on instruction (preaching in the territory).

Analyzed in detail is "Calling on people from house to house…, on streets, or at marketplaces…, at open-air markets, to taxi drivers…, street vendors, people waiting in their automobiles at shopping centers or waiting at bus or train stops…. Visiting hospitals, rest homes, jails, and so forth…. Calling on people at their places of business" (167-168).

Later we discuss extraneous amusements, such as reading books or magazines of dubious value as well as watching television or going to the movies.

I learn the answers to the following questions:

"In what ways can you support the congregation today?" (59)

"What can a wife do to make herself 'a crown to her owner'?" (52)

"Why is it not wise to rely on what we *feel* is right?" (210)

"How can you prevent the fear of working dangerous territories from becoming an obstacle to your continued service?" (192)

"Why might our listening patiently and showing consideration for the expressions of irreligious ones be helpful to them? In some instances, why may it be wise not to insist on having an extended conversation with a person who is not religious?" (250)

"Why is it good to be specific about the sins concerning which we are asking forgiveness?" (230)

"How can knowing the main ideas in the teaching of evolution be helpful when reasoning with those who accept that theory?" (252)

"Why would a Christian not oppose legal social distinctions imposed by secular authorities?"

(219)

"Why does God permit wickedness that results in severe persecution of his servants?" (236)

During one of the lessons I dare to bring up the issue of suicide. "They're Satan's thoughts. You can't listen to them. You need to pray more," explains the elder.

For a few hours in the evenings I do my homework and prepare for the next lesson. Sometimes I lock myself in the bathroom with a tape recorder. I record letters to myself: "I beg you, please, don't ever do it again. I'm begging you. Jehovah sees your hands."

I'm strong and happy. I haven't masturbated in several days. I'll leave to serve where there's the greatest need. Probably to Russia. Or I'll go to the Bethel Home to print literature. I'll find myself a wife. The thorn in my flesh, the brittle thorn in my flesh, Satan's silent angel, will finally fall out.

After the training course I already know. Not only how to talk with an atheist, a Catholic. How to address the congregation. How to encourage my close friends and family to preach more. I know most of all what the meaning of life consists of. What happens when we die. I know who I am. Why I'm here in the world.

I start to instruct my parents. They could be pioneers. They watch too much TV, and because of that I give up. "He that has greater affection for father or mother than for me is not worthy of me"

(Mt 10:37).

I instruct my brother, who withdraws further and further from religion. I regularly quote him words from the Apostle: "just as it occurred in the days of Noah, so it will be also in the days of the Son of man: they were eating, they were drinking, men were marrying, women were being given in marriage, until that day when Noah entered into the ark, and the flood arrived and destroyed them all. Likewise, just as it occurred in the days of Lot: they were eating, they were drinking, they were buying, they were selling, they were planting, they were building. But on the day that Lot came out of Sodom it rained fire and sulphur from heaven and destroyed them all. The same way it will be on that day when the Son of man is to be revealed. In that night two will be in one bed; the one will be taken along, but the other will be abandoned" (Lk 17:26-30, 34).

I conduct meetings more and more often. I preside over small assemblies. I become well known. I like admiration. I devote more time to studying the Bible. The fanatic I had cultivated in myself had become full grown.

To Ewelina the Most Important I write that if she had to die spiritually, it would be better for her to die physically. I pressure her to pioneer service. I feel smarter than my fellow believers in the congregation, than my parents, than my brother, whose contact with the worldly I was beginning to despise. I was regarded as a role model, a powerhouse.

Besides the diary and Robert, I don't speak to anyone about my pain, loneliness, about the thorn, about waiting for death that was no longer a passive hope but a longing. For Armageddon, of course.

I'm turning eighteen soon. It terrifies me. I have to—and want to—get closer to Jehovah. Today I appeared at an assembly in Jelenia Góra. I was interviewed, though I'm not worth a bucket of spit. My cousin swallowed seventy-two pills. She wanted to die. They saved her. I can't tell her that I feel the same. A pioneer can't want death.

Witnesses

A man can attain ever-higher ranks within the hierarchy. The privilege of women is cleaning the Kingdom Halls and participating in short skits about preaching. They can, like men, come forward and respond to raised questions. They can preach. But above all they should learn "in silence with full submissiveness" (1 Tim 2:11).

Women are not allowed to speak publicly, to pray, to give lectures, to criticize the statements of elders.

"Let the women keep silent in the congregations, for it is not permitted for them to speak, but let them be in subjection" (1 Cor 14:34).

If—in exceptional cases—no baptized man is participating in a meeting, then they can pray and conduct the meeting. But they must cover their head, usually with a scarf. "Every woman that prays or prophesies with her head uncovered shames her head" (1 Cor 11:5).

In the Jehovah's Witnesses' organization an extensive system of training exists.

For preachers there are three meetings a week and assemblies for field service, that is, preaching. And once every six months a visit from a traveling brother.

Regular pioneers can take advantage of the ten-day Pioneer Service School.

The introductory course for service at the Bethel Home takes forty-five minutes per week for sixteen weeks. It's intended for residents at the Bethel Home in any given country.

The Kingdom Ministry School is intended for serving men (ministerial servants, congregational elders, traveling brothers).

(Luke's dad participated in the five-day School for Congregation Elders, where he received a secret handbook intended just for them.)

There is also a two-month long School for Traveling Overseers and Their Wives as well as a Bible School for Single Brothers that takes the same amount of time. Only unmarried men between the ages of twenty-three and sixty-two who enjoy good health and have been performing administrative functions in the congregation for at least two years are eligible to participate. Whoever completes the course will be sent to remote and inaccessible areas in Poland or the world. The Bible School for Christian Couples fulfills a similar purpose.

Finally, there's the Watchtower Bible School of Gilead, where you study for five months. Classes are held in America, at the Watchtower Society's Educational Center in Patterson. It prepares future missionaries and branch office administrators worldwide. In the future they will be able to take advantage of the two-month School for Branch Committee Members and Their Wivés.

In order for a woman to be able to participate in one of the exclusive and closed courses she must be the wife of a Jehovah's Witness who fills a high position within the organization's structure.

Regardless of the function performed and their sex, followers must preach. That is their primary duty and privilege. Armageddon will come when all people will have heard about Jehovah and will have chosen the truth (life) or the world (death).

Preachers spend as much time as they can in service.

An auxiliary pioneer preaches for sixty hours a month. A regular pioneer, ninety hours, and he undertakes this task for a minimum of a year. A special pioneer (a missionary), one hundred forty hours. (It was like this during Luke's time, but in 1999 the Governing Body made changes: fifty hours for auxiliary pioneers, seventy for regular pioneers, and one hundred thirty for special pioneers.)

The most zealous are sent to particularly difficult areas, often abroad and where there hasn't been an increase of new followers for a long time.

Children are trained to preach. They often go from house to house together with their parents or other adult Witnesses.

Those who stop preaching are classified as inactive. They await their reproofing visits from the elders.

The latest methods of proselytizing are practiced during weekly classes in the Theocratic Ministry School. Almost all followers learn it. Girls and women perform in the scripted scenes. One person plays the role of a Catholic, a Buddhist, an atheist, a person who's angry, unsympathetic, or, on the contrary, interested in the truth. The task of the second person is to guide the conversations in order to convince the apostate to study the Bible. Boys and men deliver five-minute lectures from the podium based on Bible passages.

Everybody is evaluated according to the following criteria: the introduction aroused interest, clearly understood, appropriate use of Bible verses, gestures, smoothness, cohesion in applying combined phrases, inflection, enthusiasm, warmth, affection, external appearance. An elder notifies the students of their results and posts their scores: G – good, B – better, or W – work on it.

(Two letter W's are found on Luke's card next to "strength of voice" and "the use of pauses." Besides that, more than thirty G's. He had a habit of talking fast until he was out of breath, and then he'd greedily inhale and speed on with his words.)

Robert

I write a letter to the *Szklarska Poreba Weekly* because he wants to work there. It's a one-person magazine. It has only an editor-in-chief.

After two weeks he holds in his hands his first article entitled "Killing Yourself."

"But why this topic?" the editor asks.

"Suicide is on the rise. Besides, it's controversial."

The editor takes the text in his hands and reads. Luke has the courage to raise his eyes. He waits for the verdict. The editor suddenly stops, pulls out an envelope from his desk.

"Here. It arrived a while ago from a reader."

He opens my letter. He pretends that he's seeing it for the first time. The editor continues reading my text.

"Alright then. You can write it," he finally says, and Luke begins his job.

Luke

A few weeks ago I received from my parents a present that I've been waiting years for: a computer. It'll replace the Olympia typewriter with its two-tone red-and-black ribbon. I had asked for it when I finished elementary school. I kept asking till the very end. And I kept it next to the black box with the things not to be burned. Besides, since January 1, 1999, I have to preach seventy (and not like up till now, ninety) hours per month. The organization reduced the requirements in order to encourage more people to do pioneer service. I have time to write for the *Szklarska Poręba Weekly* that nobody is clearing the snow from the streets, that the public library is freezing, that some dogs bit a person. I came up with the idea for the last page of the newspaper. It's called "Factory of Emotions" and is dedicated to poetry.

In addition to the diary, I begin to keep a writing journal.

"So long, life."–January 1, 1999.

"I suffer grief one on top of the other, Philippians 2:27."–January 3.

"My first paycheck from the newspaper: 120 złoty for four pieces! Freaking awesome. Of all the people I know, it's me who has the worst character. Why?"–January 4.

"Today I picked up a packet. I'm bad, rotten, dead-tired. As if I were a living corpse. Every day I plan to change, and every day I'm disappointed with myself. I'm worthless. If not for my parents, I'd stop existing. Living. I'd like to die."–January 6. "Packet" stands for pornographic magazine. Until I get rid of it, I won't be able to pray to Jehovah. I hide the magazine in the black briefcase. I'll look at it again tonight. I put off praying.

"I passed my exams, even Russian. Before me my eighth and final semester. And my diploma."–January 9.

"I'm a rag. I don't have the courage to swallow

pills. I feel boiled. I used to be full of water. My thorn and problems were the fire beneath me. But the water's gone, and the fire's burning all the time. That's why I'm boiled. Just boiled. My head's been hurting for two weeks already. I wish I had cancer. But only those who want to live get it. Not the boiled, those who should get it."–January 14.

"I keep up appearances. I play nice. I puke with the word *I*."–January 19.

"It's night. Everybody's gone to sleep. I wish I were five again. I don't want to go to school. I don't want to know the words *Trotskyism* and *malaria*. I wish every one would forget that I had ever existed. Then I could die without guilt."–January 24.

"I feel dirty. Dirty among the saints."–January 25.

I go to a pioneer center in Złotoryja together with Ewelina the Most Important. After several hours of going door to door, we go for a coffee to be alone with each other. At night we prefer talking to sleeping.

"How terrible it is that I don't know how to be happy," she writes to me immediately after the center. "I know that if I were completely living for Jehovah then I could be happy, really happy. But I can't. It doesn't work out for me. That's why my existence is devoid of purpose, meaning, and worth. It hurts. Then I cry. And even in my outbursts I promise myself that I'll change. You know what's inside me? Emptiness. And I'm a coward, so I don't admit it to anyone. The mask that I wear on my face is so heavy I'm suffocating. I'll come to you and we'll preach. This month I'm a pioneer. Or maybe we could spend our vacation together. We wouldn't have to stop anywhere, just wander all over Poland. I remembered that you have my diary. How was it reading it?"

A few years later our joint vacation takes place, as is our custom. Every year, without our partners, we'll hit the road, only us two. And now it's night, the beginning of February. We're sitting in the kitchen over tea already for several hours, talking. I want to tell her about my thorn but I'm scared.

"Of what?" Ewelina asks.

"That you'll hate me."

"Did you kill someone?"

"No. Worse."

"The most wonderful holiday is taking place: the fourteenth day of the month of Nisan. I pass the Memorial emblems, all stressed out. Jesus gave his life for me and I can't muster a real sacrifice for him. MOP is killing me. Where is my gratitude?"– April 1.

"In the biblical sense the name Luke is light, brightness. That doesn't work for me."–April 12.

"'The fear of Jehovah means the hating of bad.'– Proverbs 8:13. I don't know what will become of me. I am Antigone. Every decision in my life will be wrong. Following after the thorn is killing me. Denying myself the thorn is killing me. I don't know which evil is worse. I love Antigone. I understand her. Like she says, she came to join in love, not hate.

Naturally, she had to die."–April 18.

"I defended my senior thesis with an A+. From now on I have my economics certificate! Wild excitement!"–April 25.

"If I don't pass my exit exams, which isn't certain at all, then I'll go to some kind of study center."–April 28.

"I passed! B in history, an A in Polish. And I'm exempt from the oral. I chose the topic: Being Human—your understanding of the essence of humanity. And even my Polish teacher congratulated me in the hallway. I apparently did better on my final than all the other part-timers. Weird. It's a wonderful feeling to have four years of education behind you. I saw Black-Eyed Ula. I miss her."–May 20.

"Robert's success! He's a poet! A letter came from *Cogito*. His poems will be published there. I'm insanely happy!"–June 11.

"I was singled out to convey greetings and to hand flowers to the principal. I walk over to her. With me are two girls. In my mind I thank her for four years of learning. I offer a flower, a yellow Gerbera. I squeeze her hand and say, 'So long.'"–June 13.

"I was in Poznan. I applied to Adam Mickiewicz University. To my dream department: elementary education with therapy. Also to architecture at the polytechnic university, and also in Jelenia Góra to Polish and to early childhood education with PE. I hate PE, but I prefer to be safe and try for these five programs. Maybe it'll work out somewhere."–

June 14.

"Inspiring absence, the madness of unconsummated sin. I'll be clean. Please go away. One of us is guilty of happiness. Not me. Again, not me."–June 15.

On July 1 I leave from Szklarska Poreba after six in the morning. In Wroclaw I board a train headed toward Krakow. I'm more than an hour late for an exam in my dream major. The essay topic: "The struggle for love and happiness or the rejection of these values for the benefit of society." The question is simple. I'm familiar with the struggle. I leave after two hours to catch the train that will arrive at Jelenia Góra after midnight. My dad's already there waiting for me. We go home. Friday, tomorrow, our convention begins in Walbrzych. For the first time I'm presenting at the circuit assembly. Several thousand people will be listening to me.

"It's 4:14 in the morning. In two hours I'm in Poznan, at the station. I wait until the day begins and go to my interview. I did well on my entrance essay. A. I'm sitting on the windowsill next to a display case with jewelry. I'm hungry. My butt hurts from the stone ledge. I want to laugh. Happiness itself has come. Such a cruelly great bliss. I watch for a few hours. I observe people like I love it. I fantasize about who they are, what they do, and why they do it. I see kings and the fallen, beggars and the cheerful, the sad and the bossy, the bitter. I see beautiful people here. I'm really happy."–June 7.

I passed all my exams. I can choose where I'll study. A traveling brother who always meets with the pioneers happens to be visiting our congregation. He reminds me that worldly studies are often controlled by Satan. He advises me to again consider whether it's better or not to become a missionary and go to Russia. And if I still want to go to college, then I should instead choose Polish in Jelenia Góra. I'd support the congregation family. Besides, with such an education, I'd be useful at the Bethel Home in their translation department or editorial office.

Despite my misgivings I choose the program in Poznan.

I spend my vacation at two pioneer centers. I'm in charge of their wrap-up. Brothers come from the local congregations. I coax my colleagues to the theater. I dress as a woman. Ewelina, as a man. We show them how to flirt while preaching. Then I slip on my sleeping bag, this time playing Satan tempting Eve and Adam. They all laugh. I shine, which is often the case in a group.

"Natalia told me that her dad's a psychologist. My mom's brother told her that I'm depressed. Great. What's more, one brother at the center said that if he had my thorn, he'd walk into a lake, since we were just at the lake. So he'd walk into a lake and drown himself. Everybody nodded, of course, yes. I nodded as well. At night I went to the lake. I walked until the water reached my mouth but I couldn't go further."–August 22.

"Ewelina wrote that she doesn't like to be unhappy. That's why she doesn't like herself. With God, it's like I'm always putting the word *forgive* in front of a mirror trying to force it to appear, hoping to find something that resembles it in the reflection. But it's just me. Knowing that nobody else knows is the worst. I'm condemned to be myself."–August 29.

"We cordially welcome you to our Bethel family! We are confident that your stay in this place will edify you spiritually and produce much joy. We have booked you in Room 3207. Day of arrival: 09/06/1999. Your brothers." My head doesn't hurt. I don't even think about MOP or the packet. Not in the house of God. Only adults, because here they can live and work by themselves. And childless couples. For several days I sweep the staircases. I help in the garden. Every day I see only Jehovah's Witnesses. I'm happy. I want to live here.

"For the removal of my thorn I'd give my computer, my own room. Everything I have. I'd live on the street. If those who are surprised that I want to die knew exactly what my thorn was, they'd stop being surprised."–September 13.

Pawel, who I've been studying with for a year, has just given his first speech at a meeting. I'm proud. Very much so. It's a good feeling to see the effects of our work, what Jehovah will accomplish with me.

At the meeting, during the announcements

about local matters, I go to the platform. In my hand I'm carrying a written-out farewell. "I remember how this hall came about in 1992. I was able to see how the happy people, longing for eternal life, fill it. Time as a human invention will soon cease to exist, and then we'll have a chance to be part of the great, shared, and happiest family in the world." At my last words I break off and bolt to the bathroom. To cry. The next day I go with my student Pawel to preach. It's his first time. Before long he gets baptized.

I go to Poznan to study.

I live in a room with my cousin. His family is all Jehovah's Witnesses too. On October 20 I become a new member of the Górna Wilda Poznan congregation. A week later I start work. Every Tuesday and Thursday evening for the next year I clean offices. First I turn on the computer and learn how to navigate the Internet. Half a year later I find out there's such a thing as a history of viewed pages. From shame I'll arrive even later so as not to meet the office staff leaving work.

My first outing with people I know from the group. Jedrek, Majka, Zuza, and Anita. We're sitting at Pod Minoga, Club Lamprey, on ul. Nowowiejskiego.

"You remind me of that young doctor," Jedrek determines.

"Who?"

"From the show. What's his name?"

"Eh?"

At Club Lamprey it's underwear night. People are dancing on the tables. I'm excited. I regret not being in my underwear.

"I know: Doogie Howser!"

"Totally you!"

And so it is. Over the next five years everyone will call me Doogie.

"Great pain. I'm no longer a pioneer. Just an ordinary preacher. I resigned after thirty-three months as a regular pioneer and seven months as an auxiliary pioneer. There were only thirty of us in the Jelenia Góra circuit out of over fifteen hundred Witnesses. Such a privilege. Now I'm turning my back on it. I feel lousy. Like a traitor. But my studies, work. I don't have time for anything. My parents said not to chase around so much. Just move at my own pace. They support me a lot."–November 24.

"I like standing right next to the tracks and watching the streetcar speed toward me. It passes by so close I can almost feel it on my jacket. Trains blow their horns. But not streetcars. I watch the light on the front of the streetcar. At that moment I feel so deadly."–December 11.

"It's getting better and better in college. A great group. And these movies in Film Club! In my psychology classes I volunteered for an IQ test. In spite of the laughter and the fact that three times on different history questions I responded Pilsudski (I like to play the goof), I scored way above average. Weird! Every deviation—even the slightest—from the norm makes me happy. My lecturers also like me. Probably because I'm such a smart aleck. I dance in the streets. Sometimes I pretend to be an airplane. Or I scream out loud. I like to walk around the city by myself. Nobody knows me and I don't know anybody. I just go, waving my hands. I already think I'll stay in Poznan forever. There's just this stupid thorn."–December 15.

"In order to keep me from becoming conceited, I was given a thorn in my flesh, a messenger of Satan, to torment me." (2 Cor 12:7 NIV).

Witnesses

In the 1960s and 70s active among Jehovah's Witnesses was the belief that school children would not live to see adulthood. Armageddon would come in a few days, weeks. Possibly years. The organization denounced not only higher education but high school as well. After elementary school, you were encouraged to undertake learning a practical trade that would come in handy in paradise.

In the article "'Temporary Residents' in a Wicked World" published in *The Watchtower* November 15, 2011, it is written: "Vigilant Christians refrain from using the world to the full with regard to higher education. Many people in this world consider higher education an indispensable stepping-stone to prestige and an affluent life. But we Christians live as temporary residents and pursue different goals. [...] Consequently, young Christians are encouraged to pursue spiritual goals, getting only as much education as is required to meet their basic needs...."

Robert

He had begun his studies more than ten years earlier, when the pressure on young people was even greater. He shocked many with his decision. They asked him, why not Jelenia Góra? Why not Wroclaw? Some place closer to home? He explained that he had family in Poznan, that education at the Adam Mickiewicz University is ranked first. But I know that he had to get away.

He wanted to study acting. Ewelina thought he'd be great at it. When they were together, they began using a certain accent, creating their own language. Before long, they could be found talking like this out in public. In college he'd be the first to raise his hand to go out to the middle of the classroom to role-play something, to take part in an experiment.

Acting was forbidden, just like all artistic paths. Political science was also out of the question. And the worst: philosophy. "Human philosophies and plans have often brought misery to the whole of society," remaining "under the influence of demonic spirits," as was written in the book *Leading Conversations on the Basics of Scriptures* in 2001. Witnesses derisively referred to philosophizing as impassioned discussions on topics unrelated to the truth.

Luke

Ewelina the Most Important is bald. A few days ago she cut off her hair. Her long, thick black hair that everyone was jealous of. I came to Bogatynia for the break. We sit on the bed in her room.

"Why?"

"'Cuz I wanted to," she answers, trying not to burst into tears.

It's February 10, 2000. I want to tell her about my thorn and she wants to know. She's a little afraid since it's got to be worse than murdering somebody. She's a little afraid. But she wants to know. I pull out my camera. I look at Ewelina through the viewfinder. She's wearing a scarf on her head. I wait to press the shutter button until her eyes are smiling. Now she takes the camera in her hands. In the photograph I'm covering my mouth with my hand, laughing. I want to tell her. For three hours I've been trying, but I'm not able to.

"Write it down."

I write on a piece of paper: "I'm gay." I fold it into a little square. To gain some time. So I can see her face when she opens it. I hand her the paper. She reads.

"Do you like Blazej?"

I look at her. I repeat in my head the first words, the question she asked. Blazej is her brother, younger than me by two weeks and two days. In my will I left him my guitar. I expected Ewelina to get up and walk away from me. Like what happens in the movies when someone goes away forever. Or to start crying. Maybe laughing. And if not, because, after all, we are friends, then to start asking me why, since when, how do I know, what does it mean. But nothing. She shrugs her shoulders and asks if I like Blazej. We laugh. I love her so much.

After break a letter arrives from Ewelina: "All of us live with the knowledge that sooner or later we'll make love, have sex. But not you. Ever. You should try." I wonder if it's better to try or to kill myself. It amounts to the same thing. I write back to Ewelina that "I'd like to cuddle someday. To hold hands. The desire is strong. I crave it a lot. And it hurts a lot. That crappy condemnation to eternal loneliness."

I go to Podolany straight from school, like every Tuesday and Thursday. Before I start cleaning the office I turn the computer on. You can still smell the scent of people and coffee in the air. It's February 17. I discover chat. I don't have to pretend to be anyone. I chat for more than three hours with strangers. I talk about myself. Later, I'm a woman, an elf, somebody's husband, a child.

When I lived in Szklarska I was never out of the house after eight. Here, I rarely return home earlier. This class, this job, this party. "Is it bad? I love Jehovah. I like these people. I feel lonely. It's once more about love," I write February 20 in my diary.

"I was in Kolobrzeg at the Mirelli Villa. I'm with her

now. She loves me. I know it! It's great. She'll come visit me. I want to love her like crazy. To talk about everything. But is she willing? Can she forgive me?" I write March 1.

Later Agnieszka shows up at the congregation in Poznan. Every so often a sister falls in love with me. I just can't. But if I could, like really knew how, then with Jehovah's help I'd for sure be cured.

I sign up for workshops conducted by Teatr Porywacze Cial, the Body Snatchers Theatre. I play a jaded suicide in an elevator, Bogus' wanker, an emotional stick. In the black box theater with blacked-out windows, barefoot, sweaty, bruises on my body from the intensive warm-up, I feel real.

Eventually I move out from my family and favorite cousin. Together with a couple of chemistry students I rent a room on ul. Šwietego Wojciecha. "First night in the new place. I decided to blow off my classes and sleep in. Nobody came chasing after me. Peace and quiet. I didn't have anything to eat. The hotplate stopped working so I ate a slice of bread soaked in water and sprinkled with sugar. Just like I used to eat. I feel terrific!"–I write March 16.

"What will tomorrow bear witness to? Will I feel uneasy in the company of brothers? Has my spirit quieted down? Moses killed the one who tormented his brother. Meek? No! Only after forty years did he become the meekest of people. Am I like a barfly?"–March 23.

"Tonight I prayed for a long time and thought

a lot. My decision has been made: I'll go to Bethel. A lot of my everyday affairs now seem trivial and stupid to me, like school and studying."–March 26.

"I'm at a crossroads. I want to go to the Bethel Home but my parents want me to finish school. What to do? I'm running out of time."–March 29.

I'm holding the pen in my hand. I want to fill out the questionnaire. I don't know what to write for the question about mental illness in my family. How to admit to a grandmother with depression and to my own suicidal thoughts? I haven't had homosexual experiences so I don't have to write about those. But the question specifically asks about your tendencies. It's required.

I give up on the Bethel Home. Instead, I fill out an application for auxiliary pioneer service in April. I have a little territory. Two apartment blocks. Poznan is well covered by Witnesses. Late in the evening, after classes and work, I preach at the train station. I tell a friend from college. The news quickly spreads. Just like the shame in my body.

"'All things are lawful for me; but not all things are advantageous. All things are lawful for me; but I will not let myself be brought under authority by anything.'–1 Cor 6:12. How great an injustice is it forbidding someone to love?"–April 6.

"I'm stuck in a dead-end. I don't feel myself."–April 12.

"I'm a fucking optimist, since I'm still living. But who am I really? In my case, hypocrisy has been thoroughly perfected."–April 18.

Robert

He was tired and frustrated. Death weighed on his mind more and more. At the beginning of his journal in 2000 he wrote, "There's a lot of buzz around the firstborn baby of the new year. Why isn't there just as much buzz around the first death of the new year? Death is disregarded."

He didn't disregard it. On the backpack that he carried to school he wrote a quote from an Ewa Lipska poem in pen: "Learn death. By heart. According to the spelling rules of lifeless expressions." He was tired of preaching and frustrated that his thorn hadn't disappeared despite his forty months in pioneer service, despite having changed schools.

"I'd like to be Robert," he wrote in his diary. "I could masturbate without feeling guilty. I could *be*. At this moment." But his favorite day was yesterday. Always yesterday. Even though Armageddon was supposed to come tomorrow.

In his journal he drew a chart entitled "Known Suicides." He divided it into three categories. In the first were found the closest from his family and from the congregation. In the second, distant acquaintances from various congregations. In the third, individuals he had only heard about.

There are sixteen people on the chart.

Seven people are dead. Rope, rope, belt, Lysol, jump, jump, insulin.

Four unsuccessful attempts: pills, pills, pills, rope.

Five have thought it through.

The most famous suicide in the Bible is Judas. He hanged himself when he betrayed Jesus. "The intentional killing of oneself is self-murder, and it is therefore displeasing in God's eyes," was written in *The Watchtower* from June 15, 2002 (30). Elders may refuse to conduct a suicide's funeral and not make available a Kingdom Hall for this purpose.

He knew that if he killed himself he'd hurt not only his close friends and family (by depriving them of their hopes of his resurrection) but above all Jehovah.

Witnesses

"You must not sow your field with seeds of two sorts, and you must not put upon yourself a garment of two sorts of thread, mixed together" (Lev 19:19).

"And in case a woman is having a running discharge, and her running discharge in her flesh proves to be blood, she should continue seven days in her menstrual impurity, and anyone touching her will be unclean until the evening. And anything upon which she may lie down in her menstrual impurity will be unclean, and everything upon which she may sit will be unclean" (Lev 15:19-20).

"In case men struggle together with one another, and the wife of the one has come near to deliver her husband out of the hand of the one striking him, and she has thrust out her hand and grabbed hold of him by his privates, you must then amputate her hand. Your eye must feel no sorrow" (Deut 25:11-12).

"You must not preserve a sorceress alive" (Ex 22:18).

"In case you build a new house, you must also make a parapet for your roof, that you may not place bloodguilt upon your house because someone falling might fall from it" (Deut 22:8).

Jehovah's Witnesses manipulate verses from the Bible just like Catholics and the hierarchies of most Christian churches by not considering all biblical commandments as binding in today's world. Those concerning homosexuality are ripped out of context to serve as a weapon. To build words and deeds of hate.

The Bible doesn't ever say anything about a loving homosexual relationship, about a union of two people of the same sex. It never comments on sex between two women, a lesbian relationship, or the raising of children by non-heterosexual couples.

The Hebrew Scriptures describe the Sodomites who want to rape the angels who are visiting Lot (Gen 19:1-11). A similar story appears in the Book of Judges (19:10-30).

The Christian Greek Scriptures maintain the

patriarchal concern for the dominant role of the man and his seed, which should only be used to enlarge the number of the chosen people.

Intriguing, however, is the bond uniting Jonathan, the firstborn of Saul, the first king of Israel, and David, who succeeded to the throne after Saul. "Jonathan's very soul became bound up with the soul of David, and Jonathan began to love him as his own soul" (1 Sam 18:1). These two lived in an extraordinary union. They made a vow to one another. "They began kissing each other and weeping for each other, until David had done it the most" (1 Sam 20:41). And when Jonathan died, David fell into despair. And he sang a mournful song to his honor: "More wonderful was your love to me than the love from women" (2 Sam 1:26).

In the Christian Greek Scriptures all three references (Rom 1:27; 1 Cor 6:9; 1 Tim 1:10) concerning homosexuality come from one person: the Apostle Paul. In the Letter to the Romans he calls homosexual acts a disgrace. The same word for long hair on men and short hair on women. The same as strife, envy, maliciousness, backbiters, idolatry, thievery, deceit, disobedience toward parents. According to Paul, all who act in this way deserve to die. All of us.

Robert

For Jehovah's Witnesses the sin isn't the homosexual tendency but rather its gratification.

The homosexual act differs from a homosexual orientation. Just like a visit to a pastry shop is different from thinking about a donut. Just like sex differs from a fantasy. As long as he doesn't visit a pastry shop, he can fantasize about a donut all he wants to. Jehovah didn't select him for salvation. Though such thoughts are certainly an abomination to God. But he has always carried these thoughts inside him, thoughts about himself that for nineteen years he didn't dare speak to anyone.

He had considered the matter. It'd be better if he were a murderer.

In the First Letter to Timothy 1:8-10, the Apostle Paul places men who lie with each other in the same league as killers. As those who murder their fathers or mothers. If Luke had killed, he would've been convicted, would've suffered a specific punishment. He would surely have been remorseful. God would've forgiven him. Maybe some people as well. Maybe he would've forgiven himself.

*

As for the Apostle Paul, I think he was gay. Whenever I'd begin talking about it, he'd order me to shut up. Because I was blaspheming.

Read it out loud again, I asked him. He takes the Warsaw Bible, because it's my favorite translation, and reads: "In order to keep me from becoming conceited, I was given a thorn in my flesh, a messenger of Satan, to torment me. Three times I pleaded with the Lord to take it away from me. But he said to me, 'My grace is sufficient for you, for my power is made perfect in weakness.' Therefore I will boast all the more gladly about my weaknesses, so that Christ's power may rest on me. That is why, for Christ's sake, I delight in weaknesses, in insults, in hardships, in persecutions, in difficulties. For when I am weak, then I am strong." (2 Cor 12:7-10).

"See?"

"See what? It's about his health problems, with his eyes."

"Or there's a little gay in him. It's insatiable."

"You're blaspheming!"

I liked when he was ruffled with a grin on his face. He wanted to believe me. On top of that, I told him that the Apostle Paul, emphasizing *apostle*, was obsessed with the idea of two men together. He alone wrote about it. Maybe he nurtured his homophobia so he wouldn't sleep with Timothy, who he tells already in the first chapter of the first letter about men lying with one another. Besides, see, I tell him—he doesn't see—yeah, see, the Apostle Paul takes delight in his weaknesses. He likes them. Insults, persecutions, hardships. It sounds masochistic, you agree, huh? If homosexuality was wrong, Jesus for sure would've mentioned it. Would've at least once mentioned it. You know I'm right, don't you?

He had stopped listening. He tuned out but took away for himself that thorn, Satan's angel. Nobody knows what the Apostle Paul had in mind. We only know that to him the particulars had become something he didn't want. In other translations it is a "goad of the flesh," a "prod." There are a few passages in the Bible that Witnesses don't understand, that they don't interpret. That they don't know about. He hid himself away there, in that little thorn, since he, too, when he was weak, manifested even greater strength on the outside, reported an even greater amount of hours, and wrote even more letters. Like St. Paul, the gay apostle.

Luke

I've come too early. I look at everybody to make sure they're not looking at me. We chatted a long time. Exchanged phone numbers. We plan to meet at the Pranger of Poznan in the Old Market Square in the evening. I wait. The phone rings. I look at the number. At that moment he walks up to me.

"Krzyš?"

"Yes."

"Ivo, hi."

We walk to plac Wolnošci, Freedom Square. Sit on a bench, talk. I'm Krzyš, a psychology student. That's how I introduce myself. I just want to talk. We talk. I won't remember about what. Ivo came by car. He offers a ride.

"Okay, sure. A ride." It's better to drive away. From the view, from the square, where my brothers and sisters might pass through at any moment. "But where to? You're not a murderer?"

"Do I look like one?" Ivo laughs.

"Prove it."

Ivo proves it. We drive to where the city ends. Some apartment blocks, next to a tree. We pull over with a view of the night. I talk. I'm talking all the time. About school, Szklarska, about educational concepts, about cleaning offices. At some point Ivo touches my neck, puts his fingers on it.

"May I?"

I nod yes, that he may. I'm talking even faster. About the fact that sometimes I wash windows at some people's houses and pocket a hundred zloty a day. About, for the most part, not having too much experience. That I go to a social work counseling workshop. And on vacation I might go take care of children from alcoholic families. Because that's all they have. Until all their stuff disappears. But my mouth is spouting words non-stop, which then form sentences and stories. There's no place for his words. Ivo has filled every space with his fingers. He's touching my neck, head. And now my ear. He's allowed himself to touch my ear. Then the neck again. He returns to the ear. It's good he's going back to the ear. It's good he's going back. I disappear. Only his touch, which I didn't know about, that it could exist, remains. His touch that has lasted already a few good years, and there's still more of this night to come. There probably wasn't ever anything besides his touch. And nothing surpasses it. Even the orgasm that will come with a yelp before midnight. I'm sitting in the passenger seat. I'm being touched and spoken to. I don't look at Ivo. I can't look at him. I look through the windshield at the night. Ivo is looking at me. I know it. I feel it. But mostly I feel his touch. In the end I don't resist. I turn my head and press against his lips.

"I'll start with the fulfillment of the body's longing. Like in a dream. Like in a movie. Like in a forbidden song about a sweetheart. Antigone still hasn't made her decision."–April 26, 2000.

"I yearn, asking myself whether I'm allowed to," I write in my journal the next day. I go for a few days to my parents. To the convention, to Diana, to Ewelina the Most Important, to Szklarska Poreba. To what I know.

I leave the house and run to a payphone, the same route I had taken when I ran away from the fire. I dial the number. I can't stop giggling. Ivo is on the other end. I run back even faster because it's hard to just stand on the ground. That moment passes like all the others. Guilt takes its place. After all, Jehovah is a jealous God.

"I hate. I hate myself. I make myself want to puke. I'm disgusting. A lack of physical complexes make up for a series of psychological complexes, if I may say so. It's exactly what the Apostle Paul wrote: 'I am fleshly, sold under sin. For what I am working out I do not know. For what I wish, this I do not practice; but what I hate is what I do.' (Rom 7:14-15)"–May 3.

I return to Poznan. I get out of the train past one in the morning. Ivo's waiting on the platform. We plan to meet the next day at Scorpio, a gay club. Sunday morning I get up early to go to a meeting. That evening I spend my first night with Ivo. In my diary I wonder if it's better to be in Polynices' situation or Antigone's. "The first night in Poznan, which was completely sleepless. Completely sleepless! Next to, with, for, on, at. It was a completely sleepless night."

I still don't know, but I never learned how to sleep with a man I desire. Every now and then I peek through my squinted eyes. Then I open them and look boldly. With the tips of my fingers I touch his skin, cheekbones. I pull back to fall asleep. And I miss it, so I go back. When skin touches skin, everything inside me rouses. I don't sleep.

I write Ivo a letter I never send: "Too bad you don't have a dog at home. I could bring presents to you and him. That'd be my excuse to go to the store for dry food, and buy vodka. And to drink for three. Then maybe right after sex you wouldn't conk out. You'd just apologize to me. And beg forgiveness for dozing off so fast."

I show Ivo my ID. I explain my lie. Ivo is sorry because he likes the name Krzyl more than my real one.

In my diary I call myself a sham of a person and on the next page I write about my love for Jehovah. Then about my infatuation, the craziness that has happened to me, that I don't call love.

We go to the movies, on walks. We always meet at his place. In the evening, lying on the bed, I read *Le petit Nicolas*. I enjoy these few minutes when

I'm alone. But I know that any minute he'll come to me, arrive clean and fragrant, come out of the bathroom in nothing but a towel. And he'll touch me.

On one occasion I meet his mom. I'm terrified of her warm smile. Ivo wants to give me a key to his apartment. I refuse. I'm even more terrified. I don't want to go to the club for Ivo's birthday party. I explain that I don't celebrate such occasions. I don't want to meet new people who'll know about me. After another phone call I agree. On the dance floor Ivo says he loves me. I break up with him after two in the morning.

"Hopelessness. Ivo isn't mine and never will be. Never. And that's just how I want it. He'll never cuddle me, make me dinner. I feel like I'm going crazy. That it'll happen any moment now. Everything's broken inside me. Why did I end it like that? I can't stop thinking about the toothbrush I left at his place and the book I didn't finish reading. But it couldn't have been love."–May 29.

I write him another unsent letter: "When I snuggled you, sometimes regret slipped in through the open window. I thought I'd lost my taste for you but instead I've lost your taste from my mouth."

Ewelina the Most Important knows about everything. She even dates a non-believer now who will become her first husband. She had decided to go to his place one night. When she returned home, her father, an elder, sent her to the judicial committee. She went. She knew she had to. "I can't be safe because I'm not without guilt," she wrote me in a letter. "I have lots of very vulgar expressions in my head as well as the names of people I love. And lots of unnecessary words shouted in anger. And even poems. To love to the point of being disgusted—it's funny! Funny? Bullshit. It's rather sad."

"I need a new personality."–June 1.

"My life is like drinking from a sieve. I lick up the moist surface and that has to be enough."–June 2.

"The red carpet is, no doubt, not waiting for me. And my grave won't be entered onto the universe's registry of monuments. There's no doubt that loving is delightful. Except it's not for me."–June 7.

"Sometimes I just bust out. I'm always laughing. Normally. Joking, acting crazy, making a fool of myself. We discussed this kind of behavior in psychology. Nobody sees me other than with a smile on my face. It's ever-fucking-lasting satisfaction. And when I'm alone, I get soaked and I'm cold.

Oh yeah! I started cussing recently.

Today I returned from Poznan. I finished my first year. My extended stay in Szklarska depresses me. The sacred stones are all covered with moss. All I know is that I can be on my own. That's all I've learned. My longing remains. Sex isn't for me. Besides, I passed my exams having a blast and not taking too much too seriously, and I still have a chance for an academic scholarship. In a few days

I'm going to a pioneer center. It's just that I feel like I'm forty years old."–June 27.

Robert

As soon as she crossed the doorstep, her father made her go confess her sins. Everything had already been arranged.

"Because you spent the night away from home?" I ask Ewelina. It's November 2014. We're sitting on her bed talking like the two of them used to.

"Yep. That's it."

"Did you confess everything?"

"I lied. I said we kissed. They asked where, on what, how many times, what I put my mouth on. On his mouth. And a little on the neck. It was embarrassing, all these questions. On the border of sexual and symbolic violence. On top of that, I managed to get two dimwits for my judicial committee."

"But they didn't disfellowship you. Were you repentant?"

"That atmosphere encourages repentance. They're sitting there in their ties reading verses with their sad faces. You feel guilty real fast."

"Was that your only committee?"

"No," Ewelina says. She starts laughing.

It was before. She was about sixteen, seventeen years old. She became friends with two sisters, twins. It hadn't even occurred to them to lie. The elders met with them at her house in the attic.

The three of them, full of contrition, sat on a mattress. The brothers prayed, read Bible verses, and then asked them about their sins. Cigarettes? It happened, but we're sorry. How many times? A couple. Not a lot. Alcohol? It happened, but we're sorry. Really. Some kind of sex? No, never. Drugs? Marijuana, but only once. Is there anything else?

"And then we got a case of the giggles. I remember it to this day. Very inappropriate, but we couldn't stop. One of them said that our laughter was strange. I saved myself with some homegrown psychology, that it was on account of the tension. In the end we confessed that sometimes we steal."

"What did you steal?"

"Oh, whatever they asked us about. Shampoo, candles. What else? they asked. Why? We didn't know. To this day I can see the twins twitching with laughter on the mattress. Then it got serious. We were repentant and apologized. They had to confer on our punishment. But, characteristically—and something you can be entirely sure about—you can preach the whole time. Nobody will deny you that privilege. In our heart of hearts that's what we were wishing for."

Followers must feel guilty. Before they believe in God, they must believe in sin. Shame, just like the contemplation of evil, is an effective control mechanism. Here is the threatening world and here are its watchmen. The greater the guilt, the greater the need for salvation. The more zealous the faith.

Witnesses

A judicial committee consists of three elders who pass judgment on the guilt of a Jehovah's Witness. It's usually preceded by an investigation—gathering evidence and listening to accusations. In the end, the suspect is interrogated. Unofficially, it's known as the Necktie Trio. Sometimes Two Neckties precede it—that is, a visit by two elders. Its aim is to support those who are drifting away from Jehovah, or those who don't attend meetings regularly, or who report too few hours, or who generally don't preach at all.

"Remember that your sin is not just against another human or the congregation. It is against God," warns the special November 15, 2006, Study Edition of *The Watchtower*, known by those who have left as *The Witchtower*.

Each Witness has an obligation to inform the elders about one's own wrongdoing as well as about the wrongdoing of his brother or sister. Sometimes a daughter denounces her mother or a father reports the sins of his child to the committee.

During the committee any question might come up. The answers serve to determine the seriousness of the sin committed.

Where did he touch you? How long? Was there an orgasm? How many times? In what place? Were you dressed? In what? What were you doing with your hands? How did she react? What did he suggest to you? Did you like it? Did anyone see you? Do you know anyone in the congregation who sins? Do you know anyone from your family who sins? Why did you do that? Are you repentant? In what way are you repentant? What does Jehovah think about you? Do you want Him to be pleased or saddened?

In *Shepherd the Flock of God*, a secret book published by the organization of Jehovah's Witnesses in 2015 exclusively for elders of the congregation, there's a list of offenses requiring the establishment of a committee and detailed instructions how it should proceed. The quotes in this section come from this book.

The Greek word *porneia* denotes the sin of immorality, debauchery, for which one should be disfellowshipped from the community. "It is not a casual touching of the sex organs but involves the manipulation of the genitals. It includes oral sex, anal sex, and the manipulation of the genitals between individuals not married to each other. [...] *Porneia* does not require skin-to-skin contact, copulation (as in penetration), or sexual climax" (59).

For a long time anal and oral sex within marriage was considered a sin of *porneia* as well. If female or male suspects don't admit guilt, if there are Witnesses who spent the night with a person of the opposite sex or "with a known homosexual," it is the basis for the establishment of a committee (61). Likewise, "passion-arousing heavy petting or caressing of breasts on numerous occasions" (63).

The one-time touching and caressing of breasts

is impure, but instead of a committee, a warning suffices.

You can sin with obscene language over the telephone, in Internet chat rooms, in letters, as well as with a lie, theft, smoking cigarettes (a single incident will be impure), by celebrating religious holidays, gluttony, gambling, maintaining contact with former Witnesses. Every time, elders must investigate the case. Sometimes the most important things are context and notoriety.

"A judicial committee is required when there is a practice of drunkenness or a single incident of drunkenness that brings notoriety," if, however, "an individual confesses to an elder that on one occasion he overindulged in alcohol to the point of drunkenness in the privacy of his own home *and there was no notoriety*, it may suffice for the elder to give strong counsel" (66-67).

A committee does not always end with a disfellowshipping. Sometimes a warning is enough or going behind them withdrawing certain privileges, like public prayer or being able to speak at meetings. All believers are usually informed of the loss of privileges or disfellowshipping in a special announcement. This is followed by a lecture on how to be on the lookout for specific, intentional sins being committed.

But when a decision is made to disfellowship, Jehovah's Witnesses stress that each time the reason wasn't because of the offense but that there was no repentance. Humbly repenting and pleading guilty are enough to be able to remain in the congregation.

If during the course of the committee the charged person threatens to take his own life, the hearing is postponed "depending upon his emotional state, it may be best to do this a day or two later" (86).

Disfellowshippings do occur in absentia. When the accused person does not want to appear before the committee or for a longer time has expressed views contrary to the teachings of *The Watchtower*, he can expect a call by an elder of the congregation who will inform him that from that moment on he no longer belongs to the family.

(A few years ago Luke's mom was summoned before the committee for brazen conduct. She had taken on the unwholesome habit of being present at meetings and asking questions, sharing her doubts. Brazen conduct is defined as "acts that reflect an attitude that betrays disrespect, disregard, or even contempt for divine standards, laws, and authority" (60). Elders constituting authority are familiar with divine standards.

Public criticism of the teachings of *The Watchtower* or of elders, expressing your doubts at a meeting, raising questions that undermine the authority of men indicates brazen conduct. It is also:

1. "Willful, continued, unnecessary association with disfellowshipped nonrelatives,"

2. "Child sexual abuse,"

3. "Continuing to date or pursue a romantic relationship with a person thought not legally or Scripturally free to marry" (60-61).

Sexual licentiousness leading to the molestation of children is for Jehovah's Witnesses the same offense as intellectual licentiousness that leads to raising questions.

After examining the case of Luke's mom, the committee dismissed it. That's probably good since she didn't feel guilty. There were times that the consequences of disfellowshipping led to the death of some followers.)

Luke

"Oh God, help me. Be near me. Jehovah, I love you. Forgive me. My life is already past its expiration date. I don't know how to live," I write July 3, 2000, the first day of the pioneer center. With me is my cousin who had tried to kill herself. There's Maciek, who's the same age as me, who draws like no one. We listen to Björk, Katarzyna Nosowska, and Radiohead together. There's Zaneta, who might be in love with me. There's Artur, Pawel, and Dawid, who I'll eventually move in with, using my own tent as storage. We're close.

It must've been about ten years ago. A gas station in Szklarska Poreba. I jump out of the car, dance in the street, run between the cars. A man filling his tank yells at me to calm down because I'm acting like a monkey on a wire. I go back to the car mad.

The saying catches on. Over the next few years they'll sometimes call me a monkey on a wire. "You hop from one extreme to the other," my dad said to me. "From sadness to euphoria, from rapture to despair."

I'm lying in my tent thinking about those words, remembering the monkey on the wire. It wasn't so long ago that he had been a man mesmerized. Now he was full of disgust for what he had done.

In the morning we pray and read the Bible. After breakfast we board a white minivan. Behind the wheel is Brother Marek, a congregation elder who also runs the center. We're going out to the nearby villages to preach. We have a songbook with us—*Sing Praises to Jehovah* with 225 songs. Everyone has his or her own favorite. Mine is "A Victory Song," number 171, sung in two voices: "Christ Jesus now rules as King, And Satan's old system totters." It continues on about Jehovah wiping away Pharaoh's army and his chariot with His right hand, and that Israel rejoiced that God was with them. That song says that Jehovah can do what He wants. The dozen or so of us are sitting in a delivery van. Everyone's singing. We laugh when someone sings an off-key note on the bumpy road. Sometimes we find the right pitch with our shaky voices. Everything's going great.

I organize the Surnormal Cabaret. In the afternoon we write the script, design costumes. In the evening we buy beer, go into the forest, light a campfire. I pitch a topic for conversation:

there is no love. Nobody agrees with me but their arguments don't convince me. Artur notes that I'm constantly yammering on about death or sex. Sure. But then both subjects are interesting. And then we touch burning sticks to the palms of our hands. Not everyone, only Zaneta, Artur, Pawel, and me.

At night I sit in my tent and write. "I don't accept myself. The knowledge of who I am hurts too much. Time could come to a standstill here where I am with these lovely people. Babes in the woods. What characters! I want to have this kind of backdrop to my life. I alone am hurting myself, I know that. I no longer have the desire to climb uphill, going with the flow is more than okay. It's finally not so bad for me. Being here with them isn't so bad for me. I closed the entrance to the tent halfway. The wind is blowing. I feel like it's embracing me."–July 10.

I want to talk with Marek, the director of the center. To tell him about my sadness, to ask for help. But the shame is too great. I confess my sins to Jehovah directly. Like Jesus. It's the first center where I'm not a pioneer. My fruit for the past two weeks is barely twenty-eight hours of preaching, twenty-one magazines handed out, twelve brochures, three repeat visits.

On July 26, 2000, I leave for Przyleg. I don't yet know that this will be the last pioneer center of my life.

Stories about demons rouse the greatest fear. We sit by the campfire. The elders had already gone to sleep.

Somebody recounts that some brother had turned away from Jehovah. He was going through a railroad crossing and the boom gate hit him on the head. It just fell on him. It fell down all by itself and killed him. And one night my mom went upstairs to the attic and got slapped in the face by a demon. Like an open-handed slap. I heard that somebody I knew had bought some old furniture from a person who conjured spirits. At night a demon started choking him. The next night it was the same, until he sold the furniture.

I'm going to sleep, to my tent, which Gaja is leaving. With freckles, green eyes, and red hair she looks like Dolores O'Riordan from The Cranberries.

"What were you doing there?"

"Nothing."

On the last evening she reveals to me that she was smelling my shirts. The ones I preach in.

August 5, a Saturday evening. Together with Pawel, the middle child of three brothers. We're hitchhiking to Strzelce Krajenskie. In town there's a music festival. We want to listen a bit, but we shouldn't. Somebody might see us. Besides, there's Dinah—the Dinah from the Bible who was raped. We bear her in mind. There's nobody at Pawel's. We order pizza. We wait for Gaja and my cousin, who, like us, had snuck away from the center.

We listen to music, talk.

After the first can of beer we go out on the balcony, and from there to the railing. I get caught on the antenna of the neighbors living below, who chase me away.

After the second can of beer I go to the kitchen for a knife. I clumsily cut my skin and paint my face with the blood.

"I don't wanna kill myself at all. It's just that—" I'm laughing because I don't want to kill myself at all. It's just that—.

I need to be left alone, to wait until the sadness in me dies down. Last year I let it rattle me. Only then I had some place to run away to. There were streetcars, cleaning offices, trips by train, trips back home from college. But here I've been around people for several days. Even at night you can hear everything through the tent walls.

Gaja is nearby the whole time asking what's the matter. What's the matter. Well, what's the matter. I lock myself in the bathroom to let out a little of my sadness. Then she breaks through the lock.

I still hadn't cried in front of anyone.

I want to tell her. But I can't through the tears, through the snot, the muddle in my head.

"I'm not crying," I say to her with a wet face. "I don't cry in front of people, but maybe I had forgotten to be scared."

"I understand everything. I already know." Gaja repeats again and again that she already knows. She brings mint tea, sits down behind me. I continue crying, in bursts. My back is hot. I remember that my back was hot. After two hours I lie down on the couch and fall asleep. Gaja is sitting at my head. She waits until I fall asleep, listens to my breath. She kisses me all over the face. But not my mouth.

She doesn't touch my mouth. She wants to hold off on my mouth because she already knows.

On August 9 I tell her that I sometimes bought myself pornographic magazines, that I masturbated looking at the guys, that I've sinned, that I've been wanting to kill myself. And she tells me about herself, how she learned the truth, how she herself had lost her virtue.

This is the crazy woman Black-Eyed Ula from high school wrote me about.

On August 12 we kiss in my tent. "Incredible chills. It's my first time. A new version. A first."–I write in my journal.

"I'm falling in love. Yesterday we kissed each other underwater in the lake. Both of us wear combat boots. But, it's well known, not to the meeting. They still frown upon us. Besides, she wears black. All black. Today we went to Karpacz. We danced by ourselves on the dance floor. We served beer to each other with our mouths. Then we smeared each other with chocolate. She still believes in love, in such perfect love. I want to believe. She accepts me."–August 17.

"If she doesn't want to end it, I won't do it either. I'll love her. I couldn't do any better. In the future we want to be theocratic punks. She knows about everything. Jehovah will help us."–August 22.

"Yes, I love her. She loves me. Tons of text messages, hot mobile phones. We'll get married in a couple of years. In July. We'll both wear white Doc Martens. She—a white dress and white bodice, a garter, also white. And I—a white suit and white shirt with a white tie. We'll rent an SUV, so we'll have a place where we can engage in legal sex immediately after the ceremony. Fast sex. Then a child, a home."–August 23.

My cousin is getting married tomorrow. Her sister and I will be witnesses. It's August 25. We're blowing up balloons, setting up tables, preparing the wedding hall in Jelenia Góra.

News comes that grandma had a stroke. I make myself another cut.

Next day the photo shoot, the wedding and reception. I'm there with Gaja. After midnight we go outside with cups in our hands and a lemon. Uncle Darek, dad's brother, has been watching me for a long time.

"Everything okay?"

I don't answer. The sadness came a few moments ago and is growing. If I open my mouth, the sadness will come out.

"Come have a chat."

We go behind the wedding hall, away from the music and people. The two of us sit on a bench.

"What's going on?"

I can't stop crying. We sit like that for more than an hour, until my tears dry up.

"Today I'm telling Gaja everything. We talk from eleven to one. Even about Ivo. About everything. I want to love. Unfailingly. I know I won't ever totally pull it off but that's okay. Nobody should want me. But she does."–August 31.

"If she, my Gaja, my beautiful, also—if she also doesn't work out for me, in my life, then that just won't be a life then. Nothing will remain. There's room for everything in this word *nothing*."–September 4.

Witnesses

In the story from the Bible, Mary must be close to the family of the young couple, who we'll never know. She gives instructions to the servants during a wedding in Cana of Galilee. The wine ran short. "Whatever he tells you, do," she says about her son, and he had them fill six stone water jars with water (Jn 2:5). Then he turns the water into wine, the taste of which greatly pleases the director of the feast himself. Jesus Christ had just performed his first miracle. And since he was at a wedding as a guest, it means that Jehovah's Witnesses can also be at weddings.

In a happy marriage the wife is subordinate to her husband and willingly cooperates with him. Even when she doesn't agree with his decisions, if they don't conflict with Jehovah's law, she remains obedient.

A wife is a complement to her husband.

A wife shows a deep respect to her husband because she reveres God.

"The head of every man is the Christ; in turn the head of a woman is the man" (1 Cor 11:3).

In a happy marriage the husband exercises his authority over his wife with care and wisdom. When children come along, the husband becomes the head of the whole house. From that moment on he must care for the family's spiritual needs.

The husband is patient and loves his wife as his own body.

The husband should not confuse subordination with absolute submission.

After getting married in a civil registry office the wedding party moves to the Kingdom Hall for a Bible lecture.

Except for pioneer centers, weddings are one of the few occasions when followers have fun, dance, live it up.

Witnesses do not raise toasts because this custom is pleasing to Satan and he may summon his demons. They don't sing "*Sto lat*" because they have the hope of eternal life. They don't greet the young couple with bread and salt, they don't smash glasses, they don't cheer "bitterly, bitterly," they don't sleep with rice or coins, don't organize an unveiling ceremony, and don't renew their wedding vows since these are pagan customs.

Wishing them the best, offering gifts, and then celebrating wedding anniversaries, however, are allowed.

At a wedding reception Jehovah's Witnesses rarely sit in chairs. Usually they are eagerly participating in the fun, games, and skits. Guests don't need to be pulled out onto the dance floor;

just about everyone dances. The music is thought out in advance—songs free of vulgar and sexually suggestive lyrics. In *The Watchtower* from May 1, 2000, we read, "If unbelieving relatives or immature Christians use vulgar or sensuous dance movements, the bridegroom might have to change the type of music or tactfully request that the dancing cease."

The organizers decide whether alcohol is to be served. It is not prohibited.

Sometimes the young couple disappear just after midnight. The fun doesn't stop. Some merely exchange knowing glances. For the newlyweds, the first, long-awaited sex. From that moment the newlyweds can live together.

Divorces are allowed if one of the spouses cheats. Then, as in the event of a spouse's death, entering into another marriage is possible.

Birth control is allowed. Sex within the confines of marriage is to be a source of pleasure and does not have to serve procreation.

Abortion is the same sin as murder or euthanasia. Followers are encouraged to make an informed decision. They decide if they'll have children and on how many. There are privileges reserved for childless couples, such as living and working in one of the Bethel Homes or missionary service abroad.

Those who decide to have children should provide them the best spiritual, emotional, and material conditions as well as raise them in obedience. "The one holding back his rod is hating his son, but the one loving him is he that does look for him with discipline," wrote Solomon (Prov 13:24). Jehovah's Witnesses have thoroughly taken these words to heart.

Robert

In the book *You Can Live Forever in Paradise on Earth* from 1982, which in the nineties was the basic handbook for studying the Bible, it is written: "The giving of discipline, even if it may include a spanking or a taking away of privileges, is an evidence that parents love their children" (245).

From that time on a brighter light poured in to the congregations on a number of issues. I'm convinced of this as well. I reach for *Insight on the Scriptures*, a biblical lexicon that the Jehovah's Witnesses published in 2006. Under the entry for *rod, staff* I find the explanation: "The book of Proverbs makes many references to this authority, the term symbolizing all forms of discipline used, including the literal rod used for chastisement. The parent is actually responsible before God to exercise this rod, controlling the child. If the parent fails in this, he will bring ruination and death to his child and disgrace and God's disapproval to himself also. (Prov 10:1; 15:20; 17:25; 19:13)" (818, vol. 2).

I want to know if he ever saw Witnesses beat their children. He did. When kids act up during meetings, they're led out to the corridor of the Kingdom Hall or to the backyard and beaten. He's heard the smacks. He usually sat till the very end. He operated the sound system, put songs on, switched on microphones. When children began acting up— and it began often, especially the little ones forced to sit in a chair for an hour and a half—the parents had to count on the heads of the disgusted brothers and sisters turning around in their direction who couldn't listen to the lecture in peace. He also saw how those disgusted nodded their heads in appreciation when a parent pulled a child from the hall. Already then the kid would begin crying. In the corridor the crying intensified. He also nodded his head at the calm imposed by violence. Those who hadn't heard the beating certainly saw how the sobbing child returned to his or her seat already quiet. It happened at conventions as well. He saw a kid led out of a crowd of brothers and sisters, beaten.

"Chill out with that surprised look. We're talking about Jehovah. The mass slaughter at Armageddon is a sign of mercy to Him," he said.

"Were you beaten?"

"What do you think?"

Luke

The urine spilled out on the floor from the bag hanging on the white metal bed frame. I had previously wiped it up with a paper towel. Now there's too much urine. It stinks up the entire room. I go to tell the nurses they put the catheter in wrong. *Bitches from the front desk, dumb front desk bitches*, I repeat in my head. It's the third time I've gone to them. Three times and nothing.

"Excuse me, I'm here about the urine," I say through the grate in the window and leave, mad at myself for that calm tone, for *excuse me*, for *about the urine*, *about that urine*—but fuck—mad at them, at the bitches from the front desk, sitting there and fucking around about some bullshit, while there's piss on the floor.

This isn't good. I feed Grandma Marta with a spoon. I don't understand how it's possible that that adored spitfire is fed with a spoon, that grandmother who always had a second helping of soup waiting.

I sit in the chair. I read in my journal to Gaja about how she beat the rug in the dorm hallway and how she worked up the homeless guys with her breasts, leaning out her window at night. She was no longer a Witness. We tell each other everything. We have to if it's going to work out. And we pray to Jehovah for help, that He'll cure me, that He'll bless us.

My dad came. Every day somebody from the family sits with grandma. We take turns. You don't leave your own. There was a place for everyone at her table, for the entire family, believers and those who had left. The only such place in a family of several dozen people.

I return home and think that I need to try, honestly.

I have to give it a shot with a woman who loves me, who writes, "I've accepted you with all your craziness. I want to be with you forever. I won't ever get tired of you. You'll be a mystery. I once was worried that I wouldn't love you like you needed and that I'd wake up already empty. I'd forgotten about that fear! Thank you."

We meet every day, write letters, talk at night. She meets my parents, who she starts calling her in-laws. They like each other, especially her and mom. When we go preach together she shows me in the middle of the street how to turn a cartwheel.

We sit in a park with a Bible asking Jehovah for help. Then we go to a meeting holding hands.

"I'll never abandon Him! Jehovah heard it. Without a ceremony I already took an oath. I'm your wife," she writes to me September 27.

The holidays are ending. I'm going to Bogatynia, to Ewelina the Most Important.

We go to a bar where you can buy fries, beer, and vodka. We order everything. In the bathroom I crack the mirror with my head. We run to the park, drunk and happy. We tear down posters hanging on the poles. Everything is permitted us, for a moment. I send a text to Ivo then I cut my arm. At home I tell Ewelina's mom, my mom's twin sister, that I'm empty inside, that I don't have anything to live for.

On October 1 I start my second year of college.

I drift off to sleep in the attic, in my new

room that you get to from the staircase next to the bathroom, mine alone. I finally live by myself. I can lock the door and open it to who I want, or pretend that I'm sleeping. When I bend down I see ul. Saperska and a playground through a small window. My parents buy me a two-burner electric stove. In the corner of my room I fix up a kitchen. My first lunch is rice with sauce from my mom. I bring back care packages, jars of grub, from Szklarska every few weeks. Jams—blueberries, raspberries, and strawberries picked by my parents. In addition to mushrooms, stuffed cabbage, sauces, lecho.

"I've been led to such a state that every day I think about you, about us. You encourage me to do many things. My life will slowly change into ours. That doesn't scare me. I'm afraid of an eternal connection," I write to Gaja October 10. And in my journal to myself I write something like this: "I know that Gaja will be the grandmother of my grandkids. I just don't understand why my brain got infected. This grave frustration—to crave what isn't for me, what's unforgivable. What fulfills. Sometimes I long for lewd shapes. Let it be someone known for only a minute or who just caught my eye. That kind of sex. I have set up inside myself a sin border. Impassable?"

Sometimes I lie in bed, lie for hours staring at the ceiling or at my hands, the movement of my fingers. These moments come infrequently, every few weeks, days. But each time they last a little longer.

I cleaned up. I even vacuumed, though I'm not in the habit. I bought champagne for sixteen złoty, a picture frame as a present. I make a salad with tomatoes and onion, cook kasha, and heat up the sauce from mom. Gaja is coming to my place for the first time.

Now I'm waiting. It's October 13, Friday. I call her my conscience, my future. The one who can give me back my anger.

I go out for Gaja at seven in the evening. After turning the key, the music is already waiting at home, in my room in the attic, with a small window that would only fit four heads. But my own window. We want to live in Gardzko. We talk about this at dinner. The long stone road, cottages scattered among the fields, next to the forest. Tranquil. We preached there over the break. Someday we'll settle in Gardzko, in a few years after our wedding.

We lie on the bed, fully clothed. I want to silence my thoughts and my body that would rather get up and leave, bored with her kisses. I'm angry at my penis that won't rise to the occasion. I don't know how I'll deal with it when I need to use it.

I go to sleep at my neighbor's, a brother from the congregation. In his basement downstairs he set up accommodations. Every night with Gaja we spend separately, otherwise we'd up at the committee.

On October 16 I begin workshops at Teatr Ósmego Dnia, the Theatre of the Eighth Day. I don't talk about it with my brothers in the congregation, only to my parents, Gaja, and Ewelina. Besides them, everyone is opposed to such things.

On one occasion we're supposed to shove the wall, reciting passages of poetry or prose. Each of us is on his own. I mix up my text. I mumble something, stumble over my words. I close my eyes. I hit the wall, each time harder. It's not working. I pretend that if I fail, Ewelina will die. I hug the bricks. I punch. I hit. I threaten and then plead. I beg. Stroke. The wall begins to shake and I finally manage to shove it a few inches. I turn around and everyone's already sitting. They had finished the task. They stare. I feel as if I had got caught masturbating.

I leave the theater with a sore hand that lasts for the next few days. I go to a meeting. I bow my head to pray together with my brothers and sisters. During the song I want to cry. I'm stupid, so stupid. The theater can't compare to my God's organization. Just to live to see Armageddon.

The next day I go to Cieplice, to Gaja and her school. She presents me as an aspiring teacher who will observe classes. I sit with her IIb class, next to my red-haired English teacher. And I'm proud of her, of *my* teacher. After school I conduct a theater workshop for students who are interested.

The thing I like most is that I can be a worm, someone who can freely do everything, blind and mute, someone who can do everything faster, that I can profess a love that I don't feel, and then hatred. The thing I like most about being in the theater is that I don't have to be myself.

"I want to tell you: avoid trying to fit in to society's mold. If you see women in the bath and then smell their dirty panties, if you drop trash in the hallway in the dark so that the old principal won't notice, if you wear on your buttocks a sleazy tattoo, if in thanksgiving you bow your head for the morning meal prayers, if at two o'clock in the morning you work up the homeless by not wearing a bra, and you drink pilfered beer, if you cry because you don't understand, because you want to, if you cook expired hot dogs in your small room and feed the dog that doesn't belong to you, like you always do, I want to say to you: you're perfect for me," I write in a letter to Gaja.

We record an audiocassette for ourselves. We talk about what we're doing, what we're thinking, where we are. We record the voices of the people we're with. She tells me to watch *Pink Floyd – The Wall* and read "Howl." She has to see *The Big Blue* so that she'll experience what it's like to want to know everything about everything.

"As for the future, I need a lot of space, freedom. What do you need? I have the impression that it's continuous contact. I'm not surprised. You're normal. Congratulations! Do you have some sort of award for normality? An abnormal relationship! I love you for being ready to be with me. I didn't feel anything today, neither badness nor sadness, neither happiness nor goodness. I lay down. I fell asleep in my clothes. My cousin woke me up. He wanted to take me to the sauna. I didn't have the strength. I fell asleep again. Then you called. It's sometimes hard for me to lift myself out of bed, to pick up something from the floor, to turn off the light. Sometimes I don't have the strength for such actions," I write to her in another letter.

November 30 I go to the movies to see *The Idiots*. At the end of the film my entire body is sweating. I'm out of breath. I lose the feeling in my arms. Then I'm not able to say anything for a long time. I'll watch this film several times, with jealousy. I could do the same if only someone would deal with my fears, even for a moment. I'd like to go to every holy place and spazz out, to spit a pastry out of my mouth, to have a serious expression when I do it. I can feel my own inner idiot who wants to come out, who wants companionship, freedom, who isn't proud of me.

On December 1 I turn twenty. I get up out of bed after two and don't do anything. In my journal I write: "Your breasts terrify me. Your eternal urge to mate. Your readiness terrifies me. And that lack of verse at the beginning of your letter. And how you crave my body, which is entitled to its rest, even when you don't entirely know me. And how you don't understand the silence, which is entitled to play between us even when we don't say everything."

Four days later during a performance of Theatre of the Eighth Day's "Dance as Long as You Can," when I hear the line "to get to know the unknown, go through the unknown," I make my decision. I don't yet have the courage to go through with it, but I already know.

I regularly go to meetings. I preach less and less.

"My gallons of tears are prayers to Jehovah. He knows everything and I think that He will help us. He hears my every pain. I love Him so. Without you I can no longer manage. Your Gaja." I answer her in my journal. It's December 12: "What I want is plunging me into despair. I recently saw three men ready for anything. It's still me, alone at night. The lover of my own hand."

On the last day of the year I board a train with Ewelina. We're going from Szklarska to Poznan. We're getting boozed up at a gay club. Ewelina kisses a woman. She wants to see what it's like. I dance with some guy. I don't remember his name, only that he smiled. It was enough for a man to smile at me for me to be interested. We kiss on the dance floor. We go to the toilet. I unbutton his pants and give him head. After a while I get bored. I want to be finished already, to stop, since the guy's not coming. But I don't know if I can, so I keep on giving him head. I'm persistent. Though it's not a very nice-looking penis. I think his penis isn't very nice-looking and my lips are hurting against my teeth from the intense sucking. "This isn't working," the guy says.

I get up from my knees. I don't know if this is my failure or success.

Ewelina and I go back downtown and dance. It's

four in the morning. We take pictures of ourselves with strangers. A New Year.

Then come my fears, anxiety, and anger, and the dreams in which over and over again somebody dies. Or I'm killing someone. They come because I'm not as repentant as I should be. Because I'm happy with my first New Year's Eve.

"I want to live, to somehow mark my own presence here. Since I was born I haven't allowed myself a vision of old age. Because of Armageddon. Now I'm beginning to think about it with hope, about all the vagaries the world will allow me. Time is preparing me for old age. And now I want to live. I can be different even with the wagging fingers. But I want to live, and without a daily newspaper at breakfast."–January 10.

January 23 I watch *Wojaczek* and *Fight Club* and I learn them by heart. I learn that destruction is the path to perfection.

February 5 I take out a policy for life and accidental death insurance for 100,000 zloty. If I died, 25,000 zloty would each go to mom, dad, Ewelina, and Gaja.

"We spend a wonderful evening together. After, Gaja wants to kiss, touch. A long time. I do everything I can. She's happy. She writes she's happy. There's a lack of willingness in me for repetition."–February 7.

I unfasten the seatbelt and roll down the window. I perch in the window and scream loudly. At the wheel is my cousin, the one who sometimes wakes me up and drags me to the sauna. It's night. We're speeding through the middle of Poznan. The three of us spent the evening together—Ewelina, my cousin, and me. We smoked some cigarettes, because my cousin, even though he's a Witness, indulges himself more and bought a pack. As it happens, I said I have the hots for guys. So yeah, I told him: I'm crazy about guys.

We drink a toast.

Now we're speeding through downtown Poznan. I'm screaming. I'm free, a little more free than yesterday. So far, three people know. The police stop us. They want to take me away to the drunk tank, for my cousin to pay a fine, as much as five hundred zloty. But he knows how to talk to the police.

February 18 I'm sitting in a meeting together with my cousin. An elder reads a passage from the Book of Isaiah 5:20: "Woe to those who are saying that good is bad and bad is good, those who are putting darkness for light and light for darkness, those who are putting bitter for sweet and sweet for bitter!" My cousin writes in my journal: "That's a pain." We continue listening to the lecture on morality.

"How do you deal with this?" I write on a slip of paper to him.

"They just can't catch you," he answers.

"But *you*, how do *you* deal with it?"

"Don't think too much."

"But I do."

"I'm coming to you for a few days," she says. "Come."

We're riding the streetcar to my work. "What are you feeling?" she asks. I hear her question. I clearly hear it and I'm responding. I want to answer her. I'm only thinking that such things aren't talked about on a streetcar. Then she starts crying.

"Have you stopped loving me?"

"No, I haven't."

"But what?"

"It's just my body doesn't know how to."

We're riding the streetcar to the Caponier roundabout. There we get on a bus that takes us to Podolany. Then we walk fifteen minutes or so. We clean the offices, walk back another fifteen minutes to the bus stop, go by bus to the Caponier roundabout and continue by streetcar to my place so we can talk.

At night Gaja cuts her arm, but not like I had done before. She cuts deeper. About a quarter of an inch deeper toward the bone. Blood drips on the floor. She cries out to Jehovah:

"What are You making us endure?!"

I write down these words because she screams them several times. "What are You making us endure." That's how she talks to God. Not *thank you*, not *please*. But with words that only pretend to be a question, that names what we're feeling.

Robert

"How do you remember Luke?"

I ask the same question to those who knew him. I'm collecting proof of his existence.

Gaja lives in England with her husband. The last time I visited her was in 2009. We went out to a gay club in Brighton to dance. Almost every club there is gay anyways. On November 25, 2014, I ask her this question. I get her email: "You have to give me some time to answer. I'll massage my scar from him. I wear it with dignity. I'll get back to you soon."

He himself said:

"The loss of a net."

"But what does that mean?" I inquire.

"I don't know how to describe it. Behind you the whole time was a net. No matter what. If you went out, whether you got up or slept, it was there the entire time. All of a sudden it's not there. Like a puppet with strings attached to his arms, legs, head. Strings that the puppet master has moved its whole life. But now somebody's cut them. It's like Alice falling down the rabbit hole."

In those days he spoke extensively about the net that had been behind his back his whole life. And now nothing. The wind. Walking in the dark.

I'm with him more often than when we were eleven and we'd meet in his room over the notebook with a gray cover. We talk more than ever. But I'm like a newborn, an impotent observer. I let him to do anything. We go to the theater together. We write his letters, his short stories together. Sometimes we lie on the floor for hours.

The very first season of *Big Brother* begins. He

sends in his application. He's so excited he can't sleep. It turns out that he was late. Once again he can't sleep, but this time out of sadness. Then he tries getting on the show *Spellbinder*. He passes the first and second eliminations. He doesn't know how to live for anything else. It has to be his live theater. He doesn't get hired for this show either.

I think he wanted to be forced into nakedness, into the truth, so that somebody would see, would appreciate him. Closed off from the world day and night with the cameras, he would've had to have burst, to spill out. He wanted that. He was exhausted with these disappointments in his life and with those things he hid from almost everyone.

On December 8, 2014, Gaja calls. She soon contacts the brothers from the Bethel Home in England so they'll strike her from the list of followers.

"I thought you weren't a Witness any more."

"I haven't been for a long time, but I never formally resigned. Reminiscing about him motivated me," she explains. "You'll get my letter tomorrow."

To Robert about Luke.

I'm sitting on my bed. I have three piles of pictures in front of me. Luke and his fan club from Strzelce Krajenskie. His admirers and numerous cousins surround him. He has a tie, white shirt, and nicely trimmed hair. The second pile is photos from running around Poznan at night, theaters, Poznan stage actors, spontaneous and happy faces. The last group of pictures are him and me at home in Szklarska. His crazy, wonderful, warm, and laughing parents. These pictures stir up sadness in me, a sense of loss, powerlessness, a heaviness that I've had to cope with day after day since breaking up.

He had the status of a prince reserved by Jehovah Himself for higher purposes. He was from the greatly respected Zamilski family known to all Jehovah's Witnesses. I was a stray. My dad wasn't an elder and my mom didn't become a pioneer. Both of them treated me like I was a lunatic, yelling and insulting me that I was joining a cult. It hurt. But I endured that pain in the name of God. That's why being in his house among his family and friends was so difficult, because that house and that family would never be mine.

I fell in love with his secret, his pain, his rebellion, his hidden second identity. I remember the look on his face when I brought up his homosexual experiences. The previous night I had been crazy. He was in the bathroom trying to slit his wrists. We drank beer, we lied to the elders. For one night we were free. Then they began talking. Notes in the meetings. I remember his studio apartment on Saperska. A table full of food and books, a double bed, unused. I slept in it alone. Luke would spend the night at the brother's downstairs. It was a Witness house. You couldn't get away from them. But maybe that's why you killed their plants on the staircase by peeing on them?

But Luke was also a messed-up kid. He hurt me. He didn't know how to kiss. He'd get pissed off and chew me out if I spread too much Nutella on a slice of bread. He was a bitchy shithead who was moody. He could change his mood several times in one day. I liked when he didn't have to play the difficult role of Jehovah's chosen one for anybody.

I was jealous of Ewelina. Ewelina with the chronic misfortune of an elder's child worked my nerves. Only now do I understand how much Luke and Ewelina needed one another.

I remember that he scribbled something in a calendar during meetings. Everybody thought he was taking impeccable notes, but he was keeping a diary! As a Witness, Luke was great at talking with people, interacting with the brothers. At meetings he was an eloquent speaker, a thoughtful, mature brother, a good role model. Everyone loved Luke. I was an exceptionally good preacher. I always spoke from the heart about Jehovah. I learned this from him. At the center we went through the villages like a storm. We'd break away from the rest of the group and sow the seed of truth, sincerely, genuinely loving Jehovah. It was beautiful and pure. We were going to get married, remember? We had set a date. Our profundity, our telepathy united us. I cried about this for a long time. Then came the pressure of everyday life and the bubble began to burst.

Luke could be ruthless and cruel. He'd bite my head off if I picked out the wrong outfit. Shabby, stretched out trousers I slipped on to go shopping with his parents. He came to the English classes that I ran. He sat in the corner, not focusing on the self-confident Gaja showing off her British accent. He zeroed in on the sexy Leszek and his incredible blue eyes.

I remember how I gradually lost my own sexuality. He didn't need it. It was an absolute problem. I hid under loose-fitting sweaters and wore big boots, grew my hair out, didn't wear makeup. I was no longer a woman. The realization that this relationship didn't have a chance came slowly. I still remember that practically all the blonds from good homes didn't like me. One time at a meeting in a Poznan hall one girl almost fainted when I told her that Luke didn't wear his wedding ring. Ego. Clunky and primitive ego. But at the time I felt like a princess, like his chosen one, his wife. And this pride in the purity of our relationship. The beginning was wonderful. We were so young.

The pain of breaking up was a physical pain. The deeper I cut my left forearm with a dull knife, the greater the relief was. And bliss, which allowed me to fall asleep. I drowned the bed in blood.

It wasn't a celibate life, like Jehovah had wanted it. It was a life without hope of ever becoming one flesh. We had to disown ourselves. It's sad that we were Witnesses then, sad that our religion had brought about such an immense, crushing sense of guilt and anguish.

I fell in love with Luke, but now I think I loved you. It was Robert who showed me the spiders in underground Poznan, told me about sex with a guy in a taxi, wrote letters, talked for hours on the telephone. You were the master of your own world that the Witnesses didn't have access to. But Gaja did!

You know Gaja no longer exists. I don't use that nickname anymore. I'm Ania the Happy. I live without God. I'm not afraid. I'm no longer afraid. I remember what you did for me two years ago. I've been sober ever since. I love you for your presence, for holding me at the time of my greatest weakness.

Namaste, brother. Your sister.

Witnesses

In the organization of Jehovah's Witnesses the mechanism of denying one's emotions, of their repression, or of their negation sometimes takes a literal form.

Preachers cannot allow themselves to express negative thoughts and feelings. Experiencing problems, they should not talk about them to anyone outside the congregation.

The congregation cannot allow public disclosure of followers' sins. It besmirches the name of Jehovah and may discourage those who might be interested.

In 2007 Lisa Myers and Richard Greenberg of NBC News in Washington reported on nine lawsuits against a policy of the Jehovah's Witnesses organization of not notifying authorities about pedophilia cases known to them. This was the case of J. Henderson, who was removed from his position of congregation elder for acts of pedophilia.

The leaders of the organization, however, never reported these cases to the police. Because of this, Henderson molested children for more than two decades.

Alvin Heard, a preacher from California, admitted to congregation elders in 1981 that he had molested three children. He was disfellowshipped from the community but no authorities had ever been alerted. He was sentenced only in 2004 for molesting other children.

In her report "Suffer the Little Children" from 2002 for BBC Television in Great Britain, journalist Betsan Powys told the story of Alison Cousin, who had informed a congregation elder that she was being abused by her own father. The congregation elder did not react, so she reported the matter to the police. Her father was sentenced to prison for five years. In the course of the trial it turned out that three years earlier he had confessed to a congregation elder that he was a pedophile and was abusing Alison's sister. He was supposed to be monitored by the organization but nothing ever came of it. No one from the congregation had warned Alison that she might meet the same fate as her older sister.

Jurors from Alameda County in California ruled in June 2012 that the Jehovah's Witnesses organization bears responsibility for the abuse of a nine-year-old girl from Fremont and awarded her $28 million. "This is the largest jury verdict for a single victim in a religious child abuse case in the country," Rick Simons, the lawyer for the plaintiff Candace Conti, said at the end of the trial. Conti agreed to disclose her identity to encourage other victims to come forward. She was repeatedly molested by Jonathan Kendrick, a fellow congregant. Jim McCabe, a lawyer for the congregation, said, "The Jehovah's Witnesses hate child abuse and believe it's a plague on humanity."

The organization has produced a number of publications about protecting children from pedophilia, which it condemns and considers a sin.

In the Governing Body's secret letter from May 24, 2010, addressed to the body of elders, one can read: "Each time when someone reports a case of sexual abuse of a child, the elders must ask for guidance from the Legal Department" in the national branch office. Informing the public prosecutor's office or the police first is not recommended. In another secret letter from October 1, 2012, also directed to the elders, this sentence appears: "It cannot be said in every case that one who has sexually abused a child could never qualify for privileges of service in the congregation."

On July 26, 2014, the international Watchtower Victims Memorial Day was celebrated for the first time. It honored all those who had lost their lives or their health as a result of pedophilia, refusing to accept blood, disfellowshipping, or other abuse of the Jehovah's Witnesses organization. People lit candles for the victims and placed cards, flowers, photographs, toys, and letters near Kingdom Halls.

People supporting the campaign were identified by a yellow ribbon.

Luke

"Bring me some drugs," I tell my cousin, the one who has the connections and who knows how to talk to the police.

He just asks, "What kind?"

"Uh, I don't really know. Just bring me something."

My cousin brings a small bag with white powder for twenty zloty. It's supposed to be thirty but there's a discount for the first order. Ewelina the Most Important is around. She says she'll look in on me, that she'll stay till tomorrow. Gaja finally left a little while ago.

"What's this?"

"Amphetamines."

"What do you do with it?"

"In your nose. Or you swallow it."

I snort half and swallow the rest. I run to the store for flowers for the brothers who I rent my room from and who live on the floor below. I trim my pubic hair with scissors and make a picture with it. Then I play *Fight Club*. Edward Norton playing the alter ego of Tyler Durden goes into his boss' office and tells him that he won't be coming to work any longer but that he'll stay on the payroll as an outside consultant. He knocks himself out with his fist. He falls on the glass table. More and more blood. He screams. The security guard comes. Edward on his knees, his boss over him. I practice the ability of guaranteeing my place on the payroll but after three blows with my fist I give up. It hurts too much. My penis has shrunk so much that I almost can't see it. Yet something's leaked out of it. And all the time I'm talking. Despite my lockjaw I'm talking nonstop. Ewelina is listening. I call my cousin to chat with my dealer. How long's this going to last and what's the matter with my penis.

"It'll pass. By now it's more than ten hours. It'll pass soon. How much did you do?"

"All of it."

"Moron, that was seven hits!"

It passes after forty hours. The bruise under my eye changes color.

"What happened?" they ask at school.

"It's nothing. I hit myself."

Later, the days come when I don't get out of bed, sometimes for several hours. I board a train, return to Szklarska, to mom for a warm meal. I sleep till noon.

I play thousand, a card game, with my parents. Dad and I are laughing at mom because she wants to help everyone. Then mom and dad are laughing at me that I'm not risking anything. After a while mom and I are laughing at dad for risking so much.

I go to the Doogie crag and tail or to the Golden View, where there aren't any people. I don't want to bump into anyone I preached to. I don't have anything to say to them. I take out my journal and write: "Show me, o Lord, Your mercy, what You deem proper, even though I didn't deserve anything. Let there be death when there's no longer anyone left for me to love. And the orgasm of two bodies. An unpaid debt because the lender was murdered. Let there also be sinful dreams fulfilled without remorse and consequence. Show me, o Lord, Your mercy, even if You call it a curse."– February 24, 2001.

March 11 I score some marijuana. I smoke it in the room in the attic with my cousin.

"Nothing's happening."

"Wait," my cousin says because he's already heard it all.

And it's not good. Every step has an echo and time grips me too closely. I have to lie down.

"If you're going to throw up, there's a bowl next to your head, on the rug," he adds and goes back home.

After a moment I jump out of bed, find the red bowl, grab it, and throw up. But the bowl disappears. It's laying nearby on the red carpet. I go over to it on all fours. I grip the bowl and throw up. Again the bowl disappears. And then it does it all once again. When I wake up after a few hours I find an empty bowl and splotches all over the rug.

I determined to try everything. Only I'll never shoot anything in my veins.

Religion had been like wearing underwear made of barbed wire.

March 17 I sign up for Big Brothers Big Sisters together with Majka and Zuza from school, who persuaded me. For several weeks we'll go to workshops that prepare the volunteers. Each of us will get a little brother or sister matched to our personality. We'll meet with them once a week for the next year to go over their homework, play, talk.

In our group is Angel, called Adam. I immediately fall in love with his eyes and his stories about backpacking along the seashore by himself. That's enough. I want to spend my life with him. And then I fall in love with Inka, called Halina. She has a shaved head and is wearing a colorful dress. There's crazy in her eyes. Both of them don't talk much. They reluctantly talk, entirely different from me. We spend the next year together. Angel, Inka, and I in symbiosis.

It begins when we find stickers in the bar from some training course. Colored circles. We stick them on our foreheads and then on everybody from the dance floor. We dance on the tables, Inka and me. Angel watches us. The three of us go back home to sleep in my bed. Inka in the middle. Nothing happens. Since Inka wants Angel and I want Angel. Angel doesn't want anyone. And then over the subsequent year we end most of our evenings like that. Inka and me together in my bed. Angel in the armchair.

It begins in Szklarska Poreba at Šniezne Kotly, the Snowy Kettles. We run in the snow in just our underwear and bare feet.

It begins in the Scorpio Club. Styrofoam balls

cover the floor. There's so many of them that you can disappear just by lying down. We don't talk. We're covered in Styrofoam and looking at each other. The night slips by until Angel says that he has to wean us off of him. He's not successful.

It begins during our regular meetings at the Tavern. Angel orders a beer. Me—a tea, because I got a joint in my pocket. Inka is drinking beer and goes out to smoke with me. Then we play Truth or Dare. Inka loses. She walks to the bar on all fours with money in her mouth and barks at the bartender. We're dying with laughter.

My cousin, Ewelina, her friends the twins who taught her to steal, and I are hiking in the Karkonosze, the Giant Mountains. It's March 24. We sleep in the Szrenica hostel. In the evening I slip half a hit of acid with a drawing of a dwarf in my mouth. The other half, under my foreskin. I'm lying next to Ewelina. We marvel at our huge feet that take up more than half the room. When we wiggle our fingers it makes a breeze that rearranges my face. I switch on the recorder. I'm taping my first ninety minutes on acid.

"Everything's crumbling, so I gotta—," I say to Ewelina.

"To record."

"To collect."

Then for half an hour we look for the differences between the words, between our feet, and between the colors of our lips.

On March 27 I buy myself a television set and DVD player, used, but in very good condition. All for 530 zloty. My cousin got the equipment at bargain price. You can count on him. Once again I watch *The Idiots*, then *The Matrix*, *Boys Don't Cry*. Until I discover *Girl, Interrupted*, which becomes a ritual.

The film begins with the question, "Have you ever confused a dream with life?" I lie down in my bed with a cigarette. Susanna Kaysen swallowed a bottle of aspirin and washed it down with a bottle of vodka. She is just asking her lover if he thinks about suicide. She tells him about becoming a new species of human: "Once it's in your head ... you become this strange new breed—a life-form that loves to fantasize about its own demise." I press pause after about an hour, when the nurses and patients of the psychiatric hospital learn Martin Luther King was shot. Only the day before he had said, "Well, I don't know what will happen now. We've got some difficult days ahead. But it really doesn't matter with me now, because I've been to the mountaintop." I'll watch the second half tomorrow. And it's like that until break, night after night, half by half.

Zuza, who I could always count on in the group, who was the first person at college I told I was a Witness, leads me out of the bar and puts her arm around me. We go home. We had met during the entrance exams because our last names began with the same letter. Then during orientation with hundreds of people we bumped into each other.

Every so often we'd bump into each other. On top of that they treated us like a couple. "Zuza, strong Zuza. She's always telling me I've changed, I've hit the skids, I'm killing myself, that she misses Doogie from our freshman year. I explain to her that he's fine, but he's gotten lost somewhere, and that I feel like recycled shit. But she only replied that I have such stoned eyes."–I write in my journal April 3.

"In corduroys, leather, smelling of smoke and alcohol, I pop in to a meeting. I leave after an hour, bored. Miš is waiting at the Pranger of Poznan. We go visit two adorable lesbians. Then to my place for tea, because he has someone. We chat until five until suddenly he starts kissing me. Nobody's ever kissed me like that before. He'll be a lover, I guess. After the past pain I can't count on anything anymore."–April 19.

April 26 at three in the morning I leave Scorpio with my cousin. We're sitting on a wall waiting for a taxi. Tall Tomek, a pilot, walks up to me and invites me to a party. My cousin doesn't say I can go but I've already jumped down from the wall.

"I'm going," I say with a laugh.

"Of course you're going," my cousin replies. He shouts to Tomek that if he kills me, then he'll kill him.

It all seems extremely funny to me.

On April 28 I head to Obrzycko for a three-day workshop with my theater group. In the evening, at Justyna's request, because she was having a bad trip, I tell her a story. It's good, from all accounts.

Then improvising a little, and we work up the idea for a new show. I'm a biceptual, a dull-witted dirtbag. And at night Kuba, Justyna, Magda, Eva, Jedrzej, and I go into the woods. We strip down naked and run up to the road, jumping in front of cars. Eventually we position ourselves along the highway, one every few yards, sticking out our thumbs trying to hitch a ride. All the cars speed up when they see us. Somebody finally pulls over. We make a run for the woods to look for our clothes.

"And what if God is dead? He can do anything so he could've killed Himself. What would happen to our world then? What would the angels do? They'd go hysterical, maybe go crazy. Would we, would people sense in that instant His death? Later? Or at all? Could he survive death and rise from the dead?"–I write that day in my journal.

I spend the beginning of May with my parents. I get a camera from them. It's one I've had my heart set on.

"I conduct myself scandalously in Poznan."

"Then don't come around here anymore," Dad says and laughs.

"Religion doesn't interest me," I reply, also with a laugh.

"You might need to go into therapy for that."

"As soon as I feel close to someone I begin asking them about everything. All too quickly I ask what's next, how he or she manages to live. I ask what's going on in their life. If its meaning has been lost somewhere. And about love as well. Maybe it's that straightforward, that everything is a result of love. I can't live here and now. Not to mention the future. Once, I lived in the past with my memories. I'd fawn over them. I won't be around tomorrow and I'm damn scared that I won't ever be."–May 18.

On May 20 I wake up having been taken for a ride and completely alone. Even my home is somewhere else. I cry in bed. I listen to Ewelina's voice recorded on the cassette. I go out to buy pills. Since it's Sunday the drugstore is closed. I walk further on, to where Rolna intersects with Hetmanska. I finally know what I have to do. There's a sense and a purpose. I remember what it feels like to know the meaning of your life, to know your purpose. It gives me peace. Immense peace. At a gas station I buy three packets of acetaminophen and two of aspirin. I already have sleeping pills and a bottle of rum at home. The rum's a present that's been waiting for several weeks for the perfect occasion. I chase the pills with the rum.

I look at my cousin, who's saying something, waving his hands.

"Everything's okay now," I smile from the bed.

"Nothing is okay!" my cousin shouts and forces salt water down me. He drags me to the toilet and tells me to vomit.

Then he hands me salt water again. If I don't vomit he's going to call an ambulance. I beg him not to because of the mandatory probation officer.

"Here's more water. Throw up already."

So I vomit. And then I sleep for almost twenty-four hours.

"God, You, who have planned out my life, You, who place before me death for my own good, You, who love in sterile conditions."–May 21, 2001.

Robert

He stopped using the name Jehovah. Just like that. Now he would've liked to stop believing altogether in God, demons, Satan. And in Armageddon.

Lying beyond a lack of faith is an emptiness more terrifying than death.

Everyone who leaves does so with the belief that the world is evil, that it's ruled by Satan. Unconsciously he looks for evil, deserves evil, expects evil. There are many dreams he needs to wake up from. A fish released from the mariculture in which it's spent its entire life will swim in every direction. It will have no idea where it's going.

"I left the door open." He explains to his cousin once again that he didn't want to kill himself at all.

"What if I hadn't come by?"

"But you did."

"I've been reporting fruit for you."

"What the fuck?"

He tells him to stop. He's furious. For several months his cousin had been filling out a field service report for him. He signed his name and put it in the mail so the congregation wouldn't consider him inactive, so he wouldn't have problems.

More and more often, when he returns to his family home, he says he doesn't believe in Jehovah, that Jehovah is stupid. It amuses him to anger his parents. Sometimes he tells them what he did in the evening, that he snorted coke and had sex standing up. But they tell him to stop talking nonsense. They don't believe a single word. For a moment he doesn't believe it himself either.

Witnesses

At the moment of death the soul dies. Jehovah's Witnesses believe that they do not possess a soul, but it's the same as with animals. They call themselves sheep or God's flock, who after death can count on the resurrection of the body if they have been enrolled in Jehovah's memory. This does not apply to the chosen 144,000 sheep that after death will go to heaven.

"Then the dust returns to the earth just as it happened to be and the spirit itself returns to the God who gave it" (Eccl 12:7).

The spirit is the life force, the breath sustaining the body throughout its life, and not the soul. Jehovah has endowed all living beings with a spirit, creating them with limitations. That is why Witnesses reject the science of evolution. At the moment of death the spirit returns to God along with the memory of the person. For followers, death is the end of existence. They do not believe in reincarnation, karma, purgatory, hell, or the transmigration of souls.

At a funeral Witnesses gather around the grave. They listen to a lecture prepared with the apostate in mind as well, who the elder preaches to on this occasion. After the lecture those gathered sing songs and place flowers on the grave. The deceased person's information, sometimes some Bible verse, is put on the tombstone, devoid of a cross since Jesus Christ was hung on a stake.

No one lights a candle. "Such customs as wake keeping, funeral celebrations, funeral anniversaries, sacrifices for the dead, and widowhood rites are all unclean and displeasing to God" is written in *The Watchtower* from February 15, 2009.

When the deceased's relatives want to conduct funeral rites differently, Witnesses may decide not to take part in them.

Leaving any sort of object with the corpse is forbidden. You must not embrace the deceased and lament because "better is it to go to the house of mourning than to go to the banquet house" (Eccl 7:2).

The belief in resurrection at times attracts to the organization those who have lost a loved one. There are special magazines designed for these people that describe a future meeting with their loved ones here on earth. Conversion always begins with building hope and the gradual dismantling of a given person's belief system so as to substitute it with the ready-made one when the time is right. Information is gradually provided by way of publications that the interested person can become familiar with.

When someone interested shows up in the Witnesses' environment, members of the congregation come up welcoming, smiling, and inviting. Nobody mentions the hierarchy, the judicial committees, the books only for men holding high positions, or the meetings reserved exclusively for pioneers and traveling brothers. Nobody mentions disfellowshipping and its consequences. At this stage you should create a new home for the interested parties. And they should live in it, abandoning their previous life and their family members who don't believe in Jehovah.

Luke

I have my head bent low, eyes clamped, and hands clenched. Brother Roman is praying for a blessing, praying to Jehovah to help me, in the name of Jesus Christ, amen. "Amen," I repeat. I had put on a shirt, vacuumed the floor. I even got diarrhea.

"This isn't a judicial committee. We came to help you."

"Okay."

They can ask about anything. I know about this from Ewelina. Even before they came I had made the decision not to lie to them even once. But I'll only talk about what I feel and not what I've been doing.

Yes, sometimes I don't want to live. I lie on the

floor. I stay there. I don't want to go to meetings. Or to preach. I feel like I've given up. No, I believe in God. Of course, I believe. Yes. Sad. Sometimes I take psychotropic drugs. (I got them from Jedrek, the model, who I can't fall in love with. Jedrek had plenty. He shared them.) Yes, I pray. But rarely. Less and less often. Okay. I'll pray more. I don't know. No, I don't know. Maybe. I don't know. I really don't know. They know. I'm suffering because I pulled away from God. If I start going to meetings, preaching, and praying, my happiness will return.

It's been two hours. I put my hands together, bow my head in prayer. In the name of Jesus Christ, amen. June 6, a Wednesday. After the pastoral visit I write in my journal, "I don't feel life." I'll lie on the floor and sleep.

The first meeting of the science club "I Feel, I Think, I Act" takes place on June 12. Me and my favorite professor came up with the idea. More than twenty people show up. I become the president and later the editor and head writer of the monthly. I'll produce it over the next few months together with Niska, a classmate from college, and who I'll eventually move in with.

I'm the first to go to the oral exam in my theory class—the impact of education. They make me because I'll improve the professor's mood.

"A-."

"But I have to get an A+. You know, academic scholarship. My reputation."

"Without flirting."

"You don't believe in my wisdom?"

"I'm not worried about your book smarts."

"You don't believe in my worldly wisdom?"

I receive an A+. We meet in the evening for wine. We stay in contact over the coming months. Sometimes through text we arrange to watch a film together, each in his own home. Then we write our impressions in one hundred sixty characters.

From another lecturer I borrow pink handcuffs.

I'm liked and still surprised by it.

I'm waiting for them to stop liking me. At any moment it may turn out that I'm leading them on, that I'm acting. And they'll discover it. They'll see that I'm dirty inside. Then they'll turn their backs on me and wag their fingers.

On June 15 I finish my second year of college and return to Szklarska Poreba.

Two tacky rings from a display are the first things. Then a book. Near eyewear, Ewelina says she'll chat up the salesperson. Unless I prefer the other way around, but this way it'll be easier. She chooses some nail polish and I look over the glasses and throw the ones I like in a shopping bag. Her friends from the congregation, the twins, had said a few months ago, "We're going to go shoplift." And she also went since she did everything they said. And then she taught me.

On June 30 I go to Brighton in England. I'm staying with my brother and his friend. After a few days I start working at Burger King at the counter. My would-be sister-in-law joins me, who later will come to my first birthday party, who I'll keep in touch with to the very end. I'm lucky to have these people.

In the morning I go to work. In the evenings I smoke hash. On my days off I wander around the city. Sometimes I'll steal something—yogurt, a jacket, fruit, pants, CDs—because I can. They finally catch me. They lead me to the back office, show the video, make me pay, and throw me out of the store.

"I pray for a touch. The fairytale of endless love no longer melts me. I just have the urge for copulation. That's a good word. Sweat on the back, a whimper, and snuggled sleep. Snuggled so tight that I wake up because of my numb arm. There's no room in it for blood. No room for circulation, we're so close. Or to sleep like an embryo, locked in someone's embrace. And then once again I return to survival mode. As soon as I feel the least little pain, creamy smoke in the lungs. I don't allow myself to fall in love, but a moment of closeness is enough for everything in me to cry out for love. The kind that's genuine, real. Even if only for a moment. Even though I know that if I had this moment I'd want it forever. I'd like to never feel guilty, to never regret."–I write August 10. I go to a small studio not far from the beach with my brother's friend, who in the meantime has become my friend. I'm getting a tattoo. At home I draw a calendar where I count down the days till I go back.

On September 1 I go to the Tavern in Szklarska

Poreba with Ewelina. I had just come back from England. Sitting next to us is a guy who I studied the Bible with a few years ago. We drink beer, reminisce.

"You appeared in the door in that black suit of yours with a Bible in your hand. I wasn't listening to you at all. I was just watching you as you talked. I wanted you to fuck me right there."

I choke on my beer.

After midnight I go to the bathroom with my former student and shut the door.

A week later I write in my journal: "I've lost my virtue. In the time it took to play both sides of the Tracy Chapman cassette. It's like I wanted, like I imagined. It's wonderful that as a gay man I can lose my virtue twice."

"I feel like I should feel stronger. Something isn't right. I want to love him. I've already heard that word. But I don't know how. Perhaps I lost my sensitivity. Will loving someone ever work out for me?"–September 13.

On September 28 I return to Poznan. After two years of general education I choose two specializations: health education and resocialization. I start studying geography as an elective. I quit after a few months and a few failed attempts to understand cartography.

I rent a two-room apartment on Casimir the Great with Niska, who I work with in the science club on the monthly journal, and her boyfriend Niski. Niska changes into a goddess, especially on

Thursdays when we drink a bottle of vodka. I like it when she changes into a goddess. She can then repeat the same sentence ten times and each time it's different.

I live in a room with Dec who's the last one to move in with us. The first evening we snort some lines and smoke some grass. Within two years we write all over our walls. With red spray paint, where the furniture stands, appears the word *ambivalence*, and further, mainly with pens and markers *look at the world from everyelsewhere, prove you're alive, take off my sock on the night train, we just had a party that goes on and on, acupunctuation, it's compatible, I'm also scared, I want a canary*. On the cupboard a quote from Philippe Quinault: "Whoever has but a moment to live has nothing more to dissimulate," and an appeal to myself: *Beg forgiveness or sin. Both together is not an option. Say: I don't know. You hold everything, except what's important, in your hands. Don't play with people with the exception of yourself. You don't have to reach the finish line or even sweat. Lose or touch.*

I sit in the kitchen, sober for two days. I don't know why I can't take reality any more—what it's like, minus the headache, painkillers, tears, and inescapable thoughts that it may simply be worse since it's so bad.

In the evenings I smoke marijuana almost daily.

I try cocaine, mushrooms, ephedrine, various drugs.

I got up unusually early, shoved a roll into my bag, poured coffee into a mug. I'll eat breakfast on the streetcar.

I draw my unspoken emotions. That's the task. Doctor Agata, the social skills training leader, makes us draw our emotions and then pair off, holding the other person's drawing so he or she can see it.

"This is terribly stupid. I don't wanna do this."

Agata comes up to me, takes my drawing.

"May I?"

With her I can. I trust her. I look at it, but after a moment I run out of the classroom. Agata comes out after me. She suggests therapy. In the drawing there was anger, great anguish, something inside me that screams a lot. This anger terrified me.

People seem to be all the same to me. Not all, but most. As if they had left a factory coming from one template. I don't know how I'm supposed to be with them. And then there's the conversations on the streetcar and people laughing at nothing. I want to grab them by the face and shout, "Why are you here?"

"I'm waiting half-stoned. There are just glasses that still need to be cleaned. Someone's chest that needs to be licked. My twenty-first birthday. My first birthday. No reason not to treat myself to some marijuana."–I write November 30. My birthday party will last three days and two nights.

On the table are evenly arranged lines of amphetamines. Marijuana in a bag. There are painkillers, beer, vodka, music. On December 1 at ten pm, the hour of my birth, I shave my head bald with a razor. Then Inka says we're invisible. We'll play this game for many months. When we're invisible, we can do anything. It's Sunday morning. We go out to a store for vodka. We go out for vodka in pajamas and through a window. Because we're invisible.

"Vomiting on a pile of freshly sweaty clothes. On my knees like a whore, rummaging through the pot in search of cabbage leaves. Spinning and spinning on the bed. Refusing to go to school, work, sleep. Saying no to life. I'm not a junkie. I'm exchanging dull sanctity for an appealing hell. Already after the first joint I detach from reality, ignoring everything except the now. After the second joint I don't understand the long, exhausting stories. The third joint—only relaxation. Which leads me to the refrigerator. It's over when I'm able to pick up the rolling papers that had fallen on the floor."

In the Jowita dorm on Zwierzyniecka you can take advantage of free counseling. I go there on the Monday after my birthday weekend. "After twenty minutes she already knows. Diagnosis: depression, schizoid states, onset paranoia, bad friends, needs a psychiatrist. What bullshit!"–December 3.

I spend most of my free time in bed. I eat in bed. I watch movies in bed. I read in bed. I smoke grass with Dec. I talk with Inka who drops by at night a few times a week.

The clinical psychology exam, one of the most

difficult. Randomized questions. Explain what dereism is. Several months ago on the wall above my bed I wrote in green: dereism. It's my word. I'm ecstatic when I write my answer. A+.

I especially like sitting in the same corner. A wall behind me, a wall to my left. I lean against it. Beside me, the most popular girl from the entire group. I lower my head over a ring binder in which there are less notes from class than unsent letters, crossed out poems, notes, drawings of people made up of several black strokes. I take out my pen and write, "Someone in front of me. A nobody, for all that. No one. Every now and then the wise voice of a lecturer gets through to me. A load of batshit crazy bullshit about the sociology of health and disease. I linger in the movements of my limbs, in the beating of my heart. I'm rooted entirely without a thought, unwittingly. Watching the same gestures, the hypocrisy of adults. Pretending to be yourself and passing, constantly performing, starting with the first person you see immediately after waking up. Nothing. Not worth anything. Worthless. To save myself, I should leave now, punching in the face everyone who ever saw me. I don't know this city or this little funny alley. Maybe it's Prague. Narrow passages, colorful houses. And emptiness. There's nobody there. It's early morning. I can see my breath. I'm walking with Robert. We're talking and listening to each other in earnest. Every word is important. Every so often we stop. We're wide-eyed, happily gawking. It couldn't be better if it were blasphemy. Some bar. A waitress as she should be. She doesn't impose herself and even has a grudge. Black, strong coffee and a cigarette. Arms crossed, on the table, joined in an embrace, everything laid out in front of us."

I haven't preached for a long time. Sometimes I pray to God but I no longer ask for forgiveness.

I don't go to meetings. Sometimes I go in Szklarska Poreba when I go back home so my parents won't be upset.

I haven't stopped believing in Armageddon and paradise. I know they'll come. And with them, death. At some point the demons will deal with all those who depart from the truth. I await them. They never show up unless they are the fear itself.

"God, make something happen. How am I to get rid of this fucking hang-up? How do I clear out my thoughts? Up — down. Euphoria — the valley, happiness — freaking out, life — death, hope — loss, expectation — desolation. And it's like that the whole time. I think it'd be wonderful if Robert walked into the kitchen now, put his hand on my shoulder and told me that nothing matters. An undestroyed, indestructible beauty has to be somewhere."–January 13, 2002.

I haven't done drugs now in almost a week. What have I got to be proud of?

I don't know anything and I don't understand anything. I don't understand the world that I've been left to live in. It's not what I signed up for. Something hurts me inside. There's no one nearby who will sometimes tell me the little lie that he loves me. Regardless, I'd still believe him.

"Since I stopped counting the kisses, the encounters, the sleepless nights together, because there's nobody, since I'm always alone and have just lied that there's no longer hope, since I'm still alive and fit for consumption, shitting, conversing, shoplifting, smoking cigarettes, a quickie in the old shitter, answering the phone, then you wrongfully condemn me to the daily question: how do you feel?"–January 29.

I've been sober for three days. I don't smoke in Szklarska. A walk through the field. A creek. Further on, a shed. A fallen tree. I had a playhouse here with my brother. I go where white roses bloom in the wild, to the foundation of the burnt house. The past is wedged up under my skull. I see me, carefree, and the maggot in my head that's been growing for a long time.

"Sobriety grinds on me like a small, sharp pebble in the shoe. One that shreds the sock, and you can't pull it out because you don't know where it is. Why is it so hard to survive an ordinary day? Sometimes I'm afraid but it's not about fear. I'd like to postpone each subsequent moment, to defer my life. Some kind of amnesia, or amnesthesia, would come in handy. My lips swell and my fingers hurt from all this suffering. Maybe it's just loneliness. I sit on the escarpment scratching them."–April 5.

When I'm sober it means that I had just woken up and that I'll soon be high. It's a new phase in my life. I had lost myself.

Yesterday we smoked a whole bag. Sleep with the too-rapid beating of my heart. So much that my orgasm was the longest of my life. I shoot for a minute.

No one has touched me for months.

"I wonder what it is that I'm continually losing, if I'll ever conquer all these addictions, and what then will I fill the emptiness with. Even now it terrifies me. Nothing makes sense to me any more."–April 16.

I go once more to the psychologist. I ask about a referral to a psychiatrist but she wants to talk. I don't say anything or I don't talk about anything relevant. I say that I heard the voice of God and now I receive something only at night. I get the referral. I walk over to the window of that bored woman. I stand there a long time. She watches me. I act out his little drama expressively because I don't trust her bullshit diagnosis. I ask if her view from here is always so ugly. Then I leave.

I end up at the psychiatrist a month later. An elderly gentleman writes several pages for half an hour. He looks at me only when I enter and when I leave. I say that I'm afraid. That doesn't interest him. He wants me to take meds. But I'm tired of their meds. Outside the door I throw away the prescription. At home they ask me what's going on. I shout and tell everyone to fuck off.

Robert

I see him from far off. On his lap he's holding a thick notebook with a green cover. He's writing me a letter. We used to meet there. He'd take only his closest friends there, to the Doogie crags in Central Szklarska Poręba. The tourists don't know about them so nobody's there.

"Robert is the most beautiful name in the world, you know?"

"I know," I answer and laugh.

"I was in love with him for almost four years. Platonically. Like on the poster, as a teenager."

"Your neighbor, the one who hiked through the mountains by himself?"

"That's right."

If a man hikes alone through the mountains it means that Luke has to fall in love with him.

"And where's your name from?"

"From the physician. The apostle, rather."

"Indeed."

He says there's no controlling time. That you can travel through it. And that moment of drowsiness is enough. The past is already molded from it, brushing aside the pain, adding a little courage and loveliness to the memorial of yourself. For this reason he writes his journal. To remember.

He summoned me out of nothing but loneliness. This place grew more and more with each passing year. The less the Jehovah's Witness was in him the louder he cried out. He loved me. So it seemed to him. I want to believe that if he knew how this story would end that he'd still think the name Robert was the most beautiful name in the world.

Luke

On May 17 they took Inka away by ambulance with the siren wailing. It wasn't necessary. She was going to be afraid of it for a long time after. She had been going to her own psychiatrist and she sent her to Gniezno. Inka agreed to it. She was in such a state she would've agreed to anything. I want her to change her psychiatrist, for her not to go to that old bitch any more. That's what I advise her.

And only a few days ago we were at the movies for *Requiem for a Dream*. Angel, Inka, and I—the symbiotic. I cried the last half hour. They carried me through town until dawn. We broke into the roof of an old tenement house—the invisible.

It takes about an hour to get to Gniezno. Along the railroad tracks poppies are blooming. They extend the whole route. You don't need to open your book. I think about how we'd meet several times a month beneath the Queen Jadwiga Bridge. We set up races. Angel, Inka, and me. Angel fired his pistol and we'd run to the wall, hit it with our head. I tripped. Inka won. She split her head open. To this day she has a scar in that spot.

I loan her my shoes with shoelaces because she wants to run in the woods. Inka gives me her flip-flops. We hold hands and run through the woods. Shoelaces are not allowed in a closed ward.

We visit Inka every few days. Angel and I, her

twin sister, and extended family. I enter the ward smiling. For a moment I belong. Someone comes up to me. Somebody always comes up. Who are you, who are you here for, give me a cigarette, what are you here for, come on, I'll show you something.

I leave and feel jealous.

I watch the people on the train. I notice how none of us look at each other. I open my letter from Inka. *My dear, soggy homeslice. You are more precious to me than many sparrows. You are a bookmark in a book I'll never stop reading. I have you whenever and wherever I want.*

1. You came because you wanted to.

2. You came because maybe you'd never forgive yourself if you didn't.

3. You came because you promised.

4. You came with hope!

5. You came because you can walk.

6. You came because it matters to you.

7. You came because you obeyed? Something! What others can't hear their whole life.

8. You came because you're named Luke—yes! That Luke.

You feel bad. I depend on you. If there's anything I can do for you, I will. Carefully. It'll take time but then it'll be okay. You have to go through it. But at the finish line there's a flower that you won't need to pick. This flower marks the spot at the end of what hurts. This flower doesn't smell but it's the kind that usually comes up during a famine. It doesn't matter how hard it'll be. Doesn't matter that you'll doubt. Doesn't matter that the majority will turn their back—perhaps you won't understand. What matters is that you came and that you got to where others were waiting for you. And then you'll find what you came for. Generally, why do you move about from place to place? You will be satisfied! Me too. As usual. There's no other way out. Inka.

After a few weeks they move Inka to a semi-open ward in Poznan. She can go out to the yard with strong Turkish coffee, sit on a bench. You never know what you'll find, what went on at night, who cried out, who they brought back, who ended up in the closed ward, maybe someone killed himself. You never know what kind of mood the place is going to be in.

"Small, dead newborns in my head. The recently deceased, the newlydeads . Questionnaires and tests. Not today, please. A large pool, a large bed, a tall tree. And, for example, little me. That would've been something. I sit in myself like I'm somebody else. How is it that one hand can pick up a piece of glass, lay it on the other hand and cut through the skin? What does the brain feel then? Is it something more than ambivalence? Why when I'm walking do I stop thinking about it and become a mechanism?"–May 27.

"'For this is what Jehovah has said: "There is no cure for your breakdown. Your stroke is chronic. There is no one pleading your cause, for your ulcer. There are no means of healing, no mending, for you. All those intensely loving you are the ones that have forgotten you. You are not the one for whom they keep searching. For with the stroke of an enemy I have struck you, with the chastisement of someone cruel...' (Jer 30:12-14)."–May 31.

On July 19, 2002, I'm once again sitting on the hard Walbrzych stadium bleachers. My last convention. I meet with Gaja. She confesses her love. And with Diana. The one from Neverland. I confess my friendship to her.

I'm sitting with Ewelina. We pass notes back and forth during the lecture on moral purity.

"Do you hear or feel anything else? Is it just indifference by now? Or maybe still the remnants of a guilty conscience?" she asks.

"I don't feel guilty any more. Someday I'll have a house with a place in it for every important person and a large parlor for all of us. There we'll find that fucking love and magic," I write back.

We spend the whole break together. We work in Szklarska Poreba at a fish and chips shop. We argue about the unwashed tables, Dostoyevsky, who she loves but I don't, about the best Radiohead song, about whether it's necessary to seek out love or to wait for it, and if it's better to wait, then for how long, about her spending too much time with her husband, about jealous me pressuring her.

"I can do whatever I want. I'm never tired. I'm never sad or angry. I like people. I accept them completely. Like mysef. Completely. I don't bully because I don't feel bullied. I like the food that's served. And every flavor of ice cream. It's me, God."–August 28.

"When I'm sitting with my mom at the table

and we're looking at each other, talking about something, doesn't matter about what, I feel that I love her strongly, that she loves me. I'll tell them. Someday I'll tell them everything. But not now, because they'd probably freak out. A hole had really opened up in the sky. You have to fight not to get sucked in. Those who are blind to the beauty are blind to the good. Please, kindly do not dictate the pieces of my life. Don't dictate!"–September 9.

"I think I'm one of those who's entitled to his loneliness, being with someone only sometimes. And only for a short time. I don't want to be right, I guess. Where are you, Robert? I'll show you someday how you were and you'll understand. You were inside me, Robert. Why me, in a sweater that's too long. Me with my stupid head, me with my lies. Why do I love you?"–October 9.

"I didn't hear when you abandoned me, God. My hope was that you'd never come. I don't understand anything. It's no longer the same and never will be. I don't understand anything. I don't want to call out Your name since you don't respond. Since you've turned a deaf ear."–October 23.

"Turning down a busy street, some handsome gentleman asks me if I might know what time it is. I do. Why doesn't he ask if we might just work out all the rest as well?"–October 28.

"I'll smoke a joint tonight. After everything I'll bow my head and say, 'I have sinned and I'm okay with that.' Is that a double sin? Pieces of my brain gush out of my ears and float around on the dry skin of my face directly onto the floor. My tape recorder also has eyes. How are you, Robert? Because for me, if you can imagine, it's a little excruciating. What's it like to be so forcefully in somebody's head for so many years and not know it?"–November 20.

On November 22 I'm sitting in a six-month study course—introduction to group therapy and interpersonal training skills. One of the directors is Martyna. I'll fall in love with her strength and sensitivity. We'll become friends later. Training takes place in Obrzycko, where I smoked grass with people from the theater and then ran naked to hitchhike. Monthly meetings begin and end in a little circle. Everyone says what he or she feels. I run out so as not to cry in front of strangers. Something awakens inside me. Everything is still blurred but on the surface I recognize my fear. And a new emotion. The directors call it sadness but I think it's probably despair. I don't feel what I feel in order to survive.

It bothers me that I'm an addict. I reinvented myself again. Lately I've been regularly faking it. I become someone I've never been before. That's precisely why I wasn't one before.

I like sleeping. My dreams tend to be understandable. Some kind of story. Complete. Even if it's a nightmare. In the daylight it's more difficult. Everything falls apart.

More and more frequently I laugh and then cry.

My love life doesn't exist. Me, gay, spurned by the marriage ceremony, unconceived children. When I was growing up, one thought kept reappearing: that I'm the only one. In a group I learn to recognize emotions. Gradually I start to love this fucked-up life.

I'll tell my parents after about two years. I'll build myself up a little. I'll tell them. Now I can be close only with those who don't condemn me and who know everything.

I'm sitting at the kitchen table. The radio is playing. I have bare feet, black corduroys, a sweatshirt with green stripes, a black tank top with Munch's *The Scream* on it. On my head a sexy mohawk. Around my neck are two masks. I like myself. It's December 12, 2002. My first day of work at Muchos Patatos. I was a bartender.

I've been sober for several weeks. I gave up marijuana.

I just conducted some workshops. They sing my praises. I'm part of the group that launched interpersonal training. I want to run away but I already know that I'm not allowed to. It's in the contract that we have to live together.

I cover my face with my hood. I cover my face with my hood because I'm crying. Next to me sits Mróweczka, a friend from college, who knows how to cry. I've been watching her for several weeks. Her presence allows me to do more.

"What's going on with you these days?" Martyna the director asks.

"I'm alone," I force out and begin bawling.

And then people talk to me. They say good things. Relief and astonishment take the place of fear.

On March 2, 2003, I complete my studies in group work skills at the Psychological Workshop Meeting. I'm booked up for the next three years:

Group Training School.

Our relationship, him and me, and even some cat.

A permanent job.

Therapy.

Admitting to my parents about myself.

Together with Mróweczka I get into an internship at the Workshop Meeting. Each week I participate in the general development classes and then I stay for the discussion with the directors. Later I'll join the staff as a trainer.

Thursday, April 24, evening, past eight o'clock. I return from an uneventful workshop. The whole time I work on my grief. Such words are used in the psychology workshops: to work on grief. I work on it, how to express it, where the prohibition of experiencing it came from, how anger replaced it, and how happiness concealed it.

I'm siting on the bed, opening a book. Mom calls. She's talking fast. Nervous. Her brother, the psychologist, a congregation elder, ran out of arguments during a quarrel. It was about the vacation home that he gave up the rights to. It was notarized, signed over to me. My grandparents' house that they bought in their old age because they had wanted to return to Szklarska a long time ago after a fire had cast them out from there. That same fire that gave me my first memory. When I was starting to drift away from the truth my grandparents drew up their will and promised to pass the house on to their daughter, my mom, who had renovated the house years ago with my dad.

Nothing will be due to those who depart from the truth.

My uncle, my mom's brother, the psychologist and congregation elder—these titles are important to me because I still believe that they are required. Therefore: my uncle, a psychologist and congregation elder, came to appreciate the fact that this house could be of use to him. Upstairs there are eleven rooms where patients can sleep and he can establish a center where he can treat addicts. For a while he'll also treat homosexual Jehovah's Witnesses there together with the addicts.

They fight over the house, over compensation. They fight in the Kingdom Hall. Mom and dad together, grandfather and uncle together. Also there, two elders in the role of witnesses. The cost estimator valued my parents' contribution at 52,000 zloty, my uncle says he'll give 30,000. There are no more arguments. But they're necessary since they're playing for money. So he shouts, shouts in my parents' faces, that their son is a homosexual. The fight is over. My uncle and grandfather win.

Mom calls me. Her brother had something like that in mind. She had to call and ask if it's true. "Is it true that you're a homosexual."

"Yes," I answer.

"What's that?"

"Yes, I'm gay."

At night a text message arrives: "Is it necessary to crawl into the sewer to determine that it's shit? Quit this shit or you'll lose us. Your parents." And later one more: "It'd be better if you had murdered somebody."

Robert

"What do you think about women?"

It's Tuesday, April 23, 2013. With this question Tomasz Raczek begins the author's evening for my debut book.

I glance to my right at my dad standing with a camera in hand. On the left sits mom. There are friends, acquaintances from the editorial board. Even my doctor came. I laugh. It might appear that I'm nervous but not really. It's an opportunity, I think. But then I start to worry. You're sitting like a faggot. You have your legs crossed. Uncross your legs. Sit with your legs spread like a real man. Don't swish with your hand. Okay. Clinch your fist at times. Good.

"You mustn't be afraid," my friend, the pop singer Mela Koteluk, sings. I had requested this snippet from her song, and she agreed. She sings and looks me in the eye because she knows.

I'm not lying. I'm not flaunting it. Those close to me know. I was at the Equality Parade. Everybody doesn't need to know. A journalist should be objective.

I know of several dozen who are in the closet. I know a dozen or so personally. An actress, actors, a musician, a singer, a playwright, film and theater directors, journalists, a dancer, a choreographer, a critic, writers, newscasters. It's not possible, until they come out, for there to be real change in Poland.

"Oh, and him."

"Also gay?"

"Yes."

"Does he have a wife?

"No."

He points out another elder to me who is hiding his sexual orientation from the congregation and from his family.

"Who knows about him?"

"His mom, Jehovah, and himself. He'll never make it to the Bethel Home. But as long as he doesn't practice his desires there's a place for him in the congregation. And if he makes just a bit more effort Jehovah will remove that thorn from him."

"And stick it in somebody else."

"Do you know what I'm most angry about?"

"That I don't have anything against gays?"

We laugh. *I don't have anything against gays.* They say such things from time to time. Perfectly smiling strangers say such things upon hearing the news that I'm gay.

Please don't ever tell me that you don't have anything against gays. That's no different from the words of those who do have something against us.

Luke

If it's true then my mom will kill herself. That thought comes to her instantly. She'll be dead before people find out. She cries like she did when she was giving birth. She sobs all night long. That's how she remembers it: she's sobbing. And she tells Jehovah that she hates Him, that He knew but didn't do anything. He didn't help. She doesn't know how she's supposed to preach now. For about a year she's certain that she'll kill herself. Before people find out. She thinks about it every day.

After a sleepless night she's sitting in the car next to dad. They have to see me. They're bringing a Bible, *The Watchtower*, and two jars of jam. They drive from Szklarska to Poznan in just under five hours.

"It can be cured," they say instead of *hello*. I open the door for them after three. Everything they know about homosexuality they know from *The Watchtower*. Dad opens the Bible. He reads aloud.

Did Jesus exist? He did.

Was there a flood? There was.

Is the Bible the word of God? It is.

Is everything clear? Yes.

They know that there's nothing impossible for Jehovah, that I can think for myself and feel what I want. As long as I don't do the repulsive things that Sodomites do. Up the pooper. That's what it comes down to. Repulsive, how can you?! And paint over this writing on your walls.

"There is no me. I am not here. It's awful."–April 25.

Sunday, two days later. I'm sitting in front a microphone. Together with Agnieszka I'm about to host our first broadcast on Radio Afera. I had seen her in the hallway during recruitment. She was sitting in a puffy skirt and chain-smoking. She had violet eyes. I had to go up to her. Every week we'll talk about one emotion, one state, one word, from two points of view. We start with fear. After our broadcast I receive another text message from my mom.

"I can't love God if He won't help you. I love you. Mom."

On April 30, at my parents' request, I meet with Brother Antoni who has been let in on the issue. Brother Antoni has been working for years at the Bethel Home. He teaches at the conventions. He oversees the development of the organization in Poland. We walk through a meadow near his home.

"Did anyone you studied the Bible with get baptized?"

"Yes."

"Then you had Jehovah's blessing."

Brother Antoni becomes sad. The matter would be simpler if there was no evidence of Jehovah's blessing. But he quickly comes up with a solution. I have to pray, go to meetings. And preach.

He picks up a rock and shows how the worms try to avoid the sun.

"These are the people of the world who surround you."

If I knew how to talk to Brother Antoni, to an overseer, the spiritual president of Poland, I'd tell him about Inka, Angel, Mróweczka, Kaska, Niska, Zuzia, Aska from Szklarska, about the girls from college, about Martynia i Beata from the Workshop Meeting, about Asia the barmaid who I work with, about Agnieszka from the radio. I'd tell him about all these people who I have loved. I don't say anything.

"You can always come to me," Brother Antoni adds as we say goodbye. "You can always come to talk."

Discussions with my parents sometimes end with me throwing my phone. The past comes back, my self-hatred. I don't want it to be like this any more.

Mom prays on her knees. Millions of times she begs Jehovah's forgiveness, that she had confessed to Him her hatred. And even more times she asks for help for her son. She asks with tears, fervently. She asks with faith. She wears out her throat with her prayers.

"The eyes get wet, but so tenderly. If someone entered my room he'd think I was yawning. I want to be strong, to stand on my own two feet. To not aid in my own forgetting. What I am actually *getting*? So I want to not just endure but to experience every day. And to remember a few days at least."–May 4.

I go to Agnieszka's for the first time. Agnieszka—from the radio. The top floor of a tenement house on Mickiewicz. There are mannequins standing in the entrance, books on the wall. In the kitchen a handmade calendar, cups on a wooden shelf, a cat and dog underfoot. On the windowsill, a photo of some people on a boat—and the most handsome man I'd ever seen.

"Who is this?"

"Tomasz."

I fall in love with the face from the photo. On my next visit Tomasz is working at the computer. Agnieszka and I are preparing for our broadcast.

"Give me your email," asks Agnieszka.

I speak loudly, emphasizing each letter. So he can hear.

On May 11 an email from Tomasz arrives. He heard. Six months later I'll be living on the top floor of a tenement house on Mickiewicz. And later we'll buy our own flat with a 35-year mortgage.

On May 12 I invite my mom to my place. I want to show her as much of my world as I can. She comes. She sleeps on the big bed in the room with writing on the walls. She wants us to go to a sex therapist.

"It's humiliating," I say.

"It's necessary," she asserts.

"But first talk on the phone."

We dial a few numbers of specialists from the phonebook. They invite mom but they're not interested in the son. If she has some kind of problem they can help.

"In the evening a stroll with the most wonderful woman in the world. She still hasn't accepted me. She doesn't understand. But at least she's gotten over the sex therapist thing. I love her. We talk nonstop. On the bed, with the newspaper, at the market, at the checkout in the supermarket."–May 14.

In the evening we eat supper, she, me, and my roommates. And then the two of us go to the movies to see *The Hours*.

On June 18 I finish my fourth year of college with a 4.0 average. I will do whatever I can to make my parents proud of me. I'll prove to myself and to them that I have a right to be.

"I like it when people look at me. Sometimes I feel proud of myself, with how I behave. That I embody the unfulfilled desires of those on their knees licking the ass cracks of their neighbors and superiors. Sometimes I almost see the finish line. And I manage to pass up my nightly chat with God."–July 4.

Two men are holding the mattress. I've been kicking for half an hour already. And yelling. I have my fists clenched. My leg is bleeding.

"Now say something about yourself. Something you wouldn't say earlier."

"I am. I'll live."

"Take care of yourself," says Andrzej, my

therapist. He hugs me for a long time.

I had found the ad in the university hallway. "Awareness and Change" training. I go together with Anita and Kacha from college. I call Kacha my half-sister and she calls me her half-brother. After the first two days of integration Andrzej invites the next person to the middle of the room.

What are you working with? Your mother or father? Who makes you angrier? Did your mother seduce you? Did you live in an emotional triangle with your parents? Perhaps there was some kind of abuse?

Then you can kick a mattress. Or fight your way out of a blanket. It symbolizes gaining your freedom. You choose which parent it represents. Andrzej encourages us to speak up about any regret. To stomp, scream. To set your mother, your grandmother, your great-grandmother before yourself. To see their message. What they've transferred to you. After the assignment you can hug him or someone else from the group. Sit on someone's lap. Everyone lies in a circle on mattresses. Some cry. "I feel like I'm beginning a new phase, that I'm dealing with myself, that I'll get a handle on myself. I wander around my essence, around my childhood. I find faint traces. There's still a lot before me. But I'm allowing myself to completely express my feelings. To cry and get angry when I need to."–July 25.

In Pobierowo. I'm lying on the beach. Next to me are Inka, Czarna, Mróweczka, and other friends. About ten people. The day before there was a blackout all over town. We danced in the street. At some point we draw a circle around ourselves with our feet, hands. A circle in the sand. If somebody goes over the line before sunset he or she will die within three days. There's enough space to lie down. When you get hungry you can call out to the guy selling corn. It's okay to approach the boundary line for such reasons. As long as you don't cross it you won't have to die. We dig out a hole in the sand so you can hide to pee into a bottle. Even those who don't believe still don't leave the circle. "The sun is beating down but the magic is already playing its part. We make sure that innocent life has not crept into our circle, that it didn't have to die. It's full of kids here. Our fatigue is increasing thanks to the sun lazily drifting across the sky. Somebody falls asleep. Crossing the line a little. A stranger. A girl. At most three years old."–August 11.

"You have created us badly, God. There's too much longing for love in us. Too much loneliness. Anyone who doesn't want to be a fanatic keeps waiting. And you're stuck in me, God, like an accusation. Like a bell around the neck because I was a cow in your pasture."–September 2.

On September 23 I participate in the next training session in Kalwaria Zebrzydowska. I've just begun a four-year psychotherapy school with Andrzej.

"I experienced childbirth today. Exhausted. I was lying there for three hours, sweaty. Under a blanket like in a cocoon. Alongside Andrzej and somebody else. I want a family and a child. I want to be heterosexual. I'll be working on that. Andrzej says that it's possible."–September 28.

In the group there are two girls with me. They're friends, devout Catholics. They love each other. During the following seminar Andrzej sets them in the middle of the room. They're separated from each other within arm's reach. You have to decide in a flash which way you're going to approach. Toward each other or toward life, to the outside. You look at each other, see what you feel and what you want to feel. The girls fall to the ground, fall apart.

"My heterosexuality is doable. I'll fight for it in order to be a father, to have a family. Andrzej asked me questions: ⁻

Do you want to be a father?

Do you want a relationship with a woman?

Is your father constantly jealous of your mother?

Did your mother choose you as the man of her life?

Do you want to be a heterosexual?"–October 24.

For therapy I unearth the first image of a man that I liked. I was four at the time.

I am looking for the pathology in how I love.

After the next session I already understand that I've been a homosexual since the time when heterosexuals become heterosexual. And I stop fighting. Forever.

From now on I demand acceptance from my parents that I myself don't know how to give them. They've got to help me. They have to accept me. They have to do it. Right now. From where I am the road seems considerably shorter.

At the master's seminar I say that I want to write about elves. I insist despite the laughter because I've always had a soft spot for them. At the next class I build on my topic: "Elves as fictitious life companions." My advisor changes it to "Fantasies and Fiction in Children and Adults." After finishing the fourth year I drop resocialization because I stop believing in it. I write my master's thesis on health education. It's about love.

After graduating I go back to Szamarzewo, there where my departmental office was. I drink coffee from a plastic cup out of a vending machine and smoke a cigarette. I'm waiting for the ghosts of my friends.

Four years after moving out I ring the doorbell to my old apartment on Casimir the Great. The turquoise paint under which Dec and I hid our writings on the walls is holding up pretty good. Later I go back twice more. But they don't open the door for me any more.

On December 29 I go to the Netherlands with my parents for my brother's wedding. He's a nonbeliever. He's marrying a non-practicing Catholic. In the civil registry office we all sit at a round table. The ceremony is short. We go to their home for dinner. We return to Poland the next day.

They call dad before the committee. By attending his son's wedding he had expressed his support for something displeasing to God.

On January 22, 2004, after more than twenty years of service to Jehovah, he loses his position as an elder of the congregation for insubordination. He lands at the very bottom of the hierarchy. Lower than the teenage boys running around during meetings with a microphone between responses to questions.

Witnesses

At meetings they open the Bible on command to the indicated place. Questions are not posed. They are known to everyone already. So after the lecturer reads a short paragraph from *The Watchtower* he right away provides the answer. As proof of the truthfulness of the spoken words a Bible passage is read.

During the lecture everyone is quiet. After the lecture there is neither discussion nor questions. That's what a Sunday meeting looks like.

Followers reject all scientific studies contrary to their way of thinking. They quote only those scientists who support their dogma and cite only their research.

With a sense of superiority they comment on the attachment of Jews to their 613 mitzvoth. They scoff at how on the Sabbath the elevator stops at every floor because Jews are not allowed to even push a button. Meanwhile, in the secret books intended for pioneers, elders, and other overseers, you can find hundreds of prohibitions for preachers. All of them obligatory.

Jehovah's Witnesses don't want to talk. That's not the reason they knock on strangers' doors. They have come to convert. They are not interested in those who are different, who have their own way of thinking. They already know the truth. Now, having been trained at meetings, they make use of all their tools and resources to lead others to the truth. They do it with a smile. Cordially. They understand every problem that troubles a person for as long as he or she remains unbaptized.

They know where we came from, what the meaning of life is, what happens after death, why we die. They know everything that's important. Every day, rather than observing, they prefer to evaluate.

Robert

He doesn't know it yet but he's just found a new religion. Psychology. He is replacing the vocabulary in his head.

Religion says once you confess everything God will forgive you. You sin. You need salvation. You are on the road to perfection.

Psychology says once you confess everything you'll be made whole. You suffer. You need help. Improve. All the time.

His new religion, professed in the liturgy of "I-message " therapy, relies primarily on the expression of emotion. Sadness means that I've lost something, that I want to get something. Fear indicates danger. Happiness is the prize. A surprise. Anger is a sign that someone is overstepping my boundaries or that I'm unable to obtain something I want, something I desire, what I deserved, what I have a right to. The I is the most important.

He saw his passion die as a consequence of talking through everything that stirred up his emotions, everything that was threatening. But his sense of security was more important.

He found tools that he began utilizing maniacally, analyzing every situation and all of the past. More and more often he got angry. He'd recognize attacks on his sovereignty in a flash. There was no such god who would have the right to harm him. He defended himself. He defended his close friends and family even when they didn't ask for it. Psychology helped in this. Thanks to it he began to realize his dreams.

He hadn't noticed that at some point getting better had become an obsession. He wanted to think through, to understand, to refine, to improve everything within himself.

At first he was treated by Andrzej. Then he had to be treated away from Andrzej.

Four times he changed psychotherapists.

Therapy helped him to experience not only his

unexpressed grief but also to experience his life in general. It helped him to cope with loss, violence, suffering. He sent all his friends to therapy.

Taking pleasure in being a victim became dangerous. In the office with facial tissue, asking about feelings, and the therapist's gazing eyes, it's easy to become one.

For a long time he didn't see that a bridge stretched between his relationship and what he didn't get in childhood. He sauntered back and forth along that bridge.

His relationship had to save him. To heal him. To nourish him. To fill his emptiness.

I will now use you, buddy. Fasten your seatbelt. In the name of love. Amen.

Luke

The cap hides my sweat-soaked hair. My robe, a recently-purchased suit. I'm standing at the podium in the university auditorium in Poznan. In front of me, more than a thousand people. It's June 19, 2004, the graduation ending five years of study. I'm not sleeping at night. On the balcony of the highest apartment in the old tenement building with a dog and a cat underfoot and my parents in the next room I read over and over again my speech written the day before.

"Good morning and a warm welcome to our chancellor, dean, faculty, parents, counselors, our friends, guests, but above all to the graduates completing their master's studies in Adult

Education, Media Studies, Early Childhood Education, Resocialization, Special Education, and Health."

Before mentioning the Health Department I pause. I look in the direction of my cohort and say, "One of the most precious assets that we had the opportunity to acquire during our time of study is our friendship." They cheer, stomp their feet, and applaud.

Others have a higher average. You haven't written your thesis yet. You speak too quickly. All this plays over and over in my head. I tell it to shut up. I take a breath. I thank our parents and look at mine. I look away because I start to get choked up.

When I finish and go to my seat, people stand and applaud. Amazing atmosphere. I'm happy. Flattered. It excites me. I'm beaming. How I like to be admired, noticed, appreciated. I soak up their praises, thinking it could've been more.

In high school my calendar was filled with the names of those I had arranged a time to preach to. Now it's full of workshops, supervision, training, and meetings with general development groups.

I describe myself as a trainer.

What works in the classroom I apply to my close relationships.

Let's talk about it. Tell me what you're feeling. Well, tell me. Say what you're feeling. What's going on with you now? I have this notion that you don't want to talk because your mom... No, that's not it. Uh-huh. It hurts. It's too personal. You don't want to talk, I understand. When you're ready, we'll talk. I'll be here, waiting. You're not saying anything. But surely you feel something. Something everyone feels. Because it's safe when I know what I'm feeling, when I know what you're feeling. Well, how do you feel. What? Well, tell me. Well, fuck. Will you finally tell me how you're feeling! Sweetheart?

During this time I regularly conduct nothing but workshops at the Psychological Workshop Meeting. I rearrange all my other work.

Every few months I take a piece of paper, sometimes colored pencils, and I plan out what I want to accomplish, to what extent, and by when. The deadline is important. I manage to achieve almost all my goals. With this faith I go into every training course, which I typically complete with the highest marks. The unemployed, ostracized women, the timid, students, senior citizens, people at risk of being laid off—everyone can accomplish what they want. Examine what you're feeling. Become aware of what you've been keeping in for years, what has silenced you. Express it. You have my support. I'm here for you. Now draw, write where you want to go. You'll succeed.

"I need freedom so I won't become a lifeless zombie, so I don't need to dissociate myself from what I'm feeling, what I have a right to. I don't consider myself guilty. I know who I am. I know how to ask for help. I have discovered my private depths. I'm not afraid of those depths or of anything I'm feeling. I no longer pressure myself to perform, to deceive others and myself. I've guided myself to the world."–I write in my journal on December 12, 2004.

I call myself an atheist.

"Jehovah is dead," I tell my parents when I'm with them at their home. "Jehovah is a cruel and stupid god. He doesn't care what I do with my penis."

I like to damage their faith. To take revenge for the heritage I received.

I sign up for the former Jehovah's Witness forum. I find understanding and a community there. My unique experiences turn out to be universal. When I learn that in addition to the public group there's an internal group for the most dedicated users, I leave.

A lot of former Jehovah's Witnesses make their lack of faith in Jehovah their new faith. Their obsession with proving the errors of the religion, their hotheadedness in discussion, their desire to discourage believers from their faith remind me of myself from when I was a pioneer.

The practice of atheism is a religion that I also abandon.

On January 25, 2008, I send a letter to the Bethel Home and my own congregation. From that moment on I was no longer a Jehovah's Witness.

"My decision is a conscious choice to leave the religion that I consider false, believing in God all the time." What's more, I go on for two pages about their discrimination of women, violence against children, the constant changes in position concerning the end of the world, the hierarchy, the secret books, the hypocrisy, the financial exploitation, the manipulation, the psychological instruments of pressure, and many other issues. The letter ends with me requesting that it be read at the meeting "during the announcement about my disassociation from the organization. I am aware, however, that this request may not be carried out since encouraging followers to think for themselves threatens the religion of Jehovah's Witnesses. Sincerely, Luke Zamilski."

The letter was never read publicly.

In 2009 I receive the highest level of recommendation awarded to trainers by the Polish Psychological Association.

After each day of the training course I go back home, content and worn out, often touched by something that happened. I feel like an expert on myself and the people around me, an expert on relationships. My own—after six years together, one home, and one dog—falls apart in a few months.

I abandon a lot of people and the city.

I move to Wroclaw to live with Ewelina who had just gotten divorced. We create a home.

I begin writing.

My entire family is standing over the coffin. No one

from the outside can see that we're standing in two groups. Witnesses together and together those who have left. The elder's speech comes to an end.

The body of my grandmother who I had visited in the hospital lies covered with soil.

I go up to my cousin, the one who I went to the centers with, who I didn't dare tell that I knew what it was like to want to die. I approach her with an outstretched hand. My cousin looks at me and says, "You know the rules." I walk away.

I still try with my aunt, Diana's mother. She doesn't offer me her hand either.

And still one more aunt. I loved her not so very long ago and very strongly. She turns her back and goes to her husband.

I return to my parents. I'm fortunate to have them. Contrary to what the organization demands they haven't disowned their unbelieving sons.

Witnesses

Disfellowshipped people are worse than people of the world. Jehovah's Witnesses can't so much as say *good morning* to them. Literally.

The disfellowshipped can go to meetings but no one is allowed to talk to them. If a Jehovah's Witness finds himself with some such person in the same means of transportation, he should not interact with the disfellowshipped. Even if it is a car. Even if everyone in that car is going to a meeting.

Whoever independently decides to leave

the religion acquires the same status as the disfellowshipped. A Jehovah's Witness who willfully maintains contact with a disfellowshipped person risks becoming disfellowshipped himself.

How to deal with former followers is already set down in the secret Jehovah's Witness book *Shepherd the Flock of God*, from which the following quotations come.

Not every sinner is disfellowshipped. Exhibiting remorse, they become marked. It is the slightest form of punishment. You can become marked, for example, by dating or being friends with someone outside the congregation.

The marked are given a warning talk at the Kingdom Hall. "If the disorderly one becomes ashamed of his ways and is moved to change, then as elders of the congregation see the adjustment, they can individually decide to end the limitation they have put on personally socializing with him. This will indicate to the congregation that he is no longer marked" (125).

A spiritual bond is superior to the familial.

The parents whose adult children have been disfellowshipped are advised to sever ties with them. "Although there might be a need for limited contact on some rare occasion to care for a necessary family matter, any such contact should be kept to a minimum" (from the section "How to Treat a Disfellowshipped Person" in *God's Love*).

Family members who maintain their contact with the disfellowshipped can expect an admonishing talk from congregational elders. But when family members live under one roof with a disfellowshipped person, they will not be summoned to a committee for maintaining contact with him or her.

Jehovah's Witnesses have their own interpretation of the law concerning the protection of personal data. "Once a year the body of elders reviews a list of those in the congregation territory who are disfellowshipped or disassociated. They will call on each one they select in order to see if he wants to return" (114). When a disfellowshipped person moves, the elders "should not send his *Congregation's Publisher Record* (S-21) cards or the confidential file to the congregation where he lives or attends meetings" (114). The documents of such a person are to remain in his or her family congregation. "However, a brief letter should be sent to the body of elders in whose territory he lives to inform them that a disfellowshipped or disassociated person lives in their territory and to provide his address" (115).

Elders do not visit apostates. The disfellowshipped who speak ill of the Jehovah's Witness religion belong to this group. Those who have left call the contradictory views on one's obligations within the organization *thoughtcrimes*. Those disfellowshipped for criticizing the teachings of *The Watchtower* are treated just like those disfellowshipped due to a lack of remorse for their sin of murder.

Every few days or weeks in a forum about Jehovah's Witnesses (www.watchtower-forum. pl) in the section "*Moja historia*" ["My Story"] you can read through the stories of those who had been separated by the religion, of those whose immediate family it had taken away. There is a mother's letter, desperate. For years she's been waiting for her daughter who broke off all contact with her. Each story is different but the mechanism for the production of pain is the same.

The disfellowshipped typically have no place to go. They lose everything they knew. And everyone they knew. Even if what was known had been an illusion, it offered a sense of security. What awaits the disfellowshipped is alien. It's the beginning of a very lonely world. They should suffer and be sorry. It has to arouse a longing and a desire to return to the organization.

Disfellowshipping "preserves the congregation's spiritual cleanness," as it is stated in *The Watchtower* from November 15, 2006 (27).

The disfellowshipped usually prefer to be called *liberated*.

Luke

It's December 24, 2004. I'm the last to leave from work. At the milk bar I make a point of ordering red borscht. It's what a Pole would eat for Wigilia. For once I pretend to be a normal Pole. I don't want to go to Szklarska, to pretend that Christmas is an ordinary day. Most of my loved ones, those who I've chosen, are already sitting at prepared tables with presents sitting nearby. I want to punish my parents for having deprived me of Santa Claus. In the same way they were punished long ago by their parents. And now they are being punished by me, their son, who denies them his presence. But I don't think about that. My pain is foremost. It eclipses everything.

On ul. Fredry in Poznań stands a red brick church. The heavy doors yield to my hand. I look around and walk over to the confessional. I kneel like they kneel in the movies.

"Hello."

"..."

"Hello, I've never been here before. What should I do first?"

"Please turn off your music," says the priest. He must've heard the sound coming from my headphones. Embarrassed, I turn off my mp3 player.

"Now what?"

"Now please spit out your gum."

I've started off great, I think to myself. But at least embarrassment takes the place of my fear.

"I'm not Catholic. I grew up in a family of Jehovah's Witnesses."

"Uh, let's step outside in front of the church."

We go out. The baffled priest looks at me for a long time. He must see from my face that I didn't come here as a joke. He suggests I find a community of Christians near where I live. He's in a hurry. Mass is starting.

"First you need to be baptized, then confirmation. And only then can you come to confession," he says as a farewell.

Earlier I had already made up my mind to do Wigilia by myself. Kacha my half-sister is coming. I even bought hay. I laid it out under the tablecloth. There are twelve dishes since we're also counting butter and bread. Borscht from a packet, but delicious. A Christmas tree. Presents beneath it. Since it's my first Wigilia it has to be proper. Kacha helps out.

And then I'm going to my Tomasz's home, to the in-laws. I'll spend Wigilias with them over the next few years. Three days full of eating, drinking, taking walks, reading books, watching stupid movies, conversations about important things and about nothing. It's better than I had imagined.

For a few years I'll return to the church on Fedry on Wigilia to sit on the pew.

When I live in Warsaw I'll go to the Camaldolese Church in the Bielanski Forest. After mass you can pet the donkey, buy a pastry in the basement, talk with the priest.

I'll look for the truth among Buddhists, in their community and in their freedom.

In the Protestant Church of Glory I experience the greatest joy that can happen during prayer.

A Zen master will teach me meditation.

In a yarmulke I will find God beneath my fingers

on the hard warm stones at the Western Wall.

I will marvel at the irony and cynicism of agnostics.

I will allow the laying on of hands of those who speak in tongues and of those who heal with energy.

These journeys will be built from my encounters with believers. I will have a soft spot for them to the very end.

I'm packing my sheets, blanket, clothes. I look at my books, I won't need them. Just like my laptop, cell phone, money, notepad, pen, and music. It's October 23, 2012. I'm heading to Krutynia in the Masurian Lake District, where I will die even though I had planned something entirely different for myself.

Robert

I'm sitting at his desk. On the right is a thin wooden cross. He got it from a friend in Assisi when they visited the Basilica of Saint Francis. The cross is laying next to a smiling Buddha made from green stone. There's also three minerals from Celtic witches. They heal. A rosary from Bethlehem. Bastet, the cat goddess of love, and an ankh, a fertility cross from Egypt. A stone pyramid that emanates pure energy. A 9 embedded in cut shells—a good-luck charm from Thailand. A red-and-white lighthouse—an ancient goddess of love.

He had been ready for a long time. He became more

and more transparent, prone to being torn apart. It happened on the sixth day during a meditation retreat at the Vipassana training course at Krutynia in the Masurian Lake District. You don't have to be a member to go there. You don't have to believe.

The pain came quickly during one of the hours of motionless meditation. Luke was punctilious. He didn't move so much as a finger. If it itched, then it itched. Like hell. And it was painful. Like it was on fire and aching. He observed. The pain came from his left foot. The cramp turned into a throbbing. Then into a stinging that moved around his calf up to his thigh. Breathe in, breathe out. Pain. Breathe in, breathe out. Pain. Breathe in, breathe out. Stillness. *Whatever happens*, he told himself, he told his body, *whatever happens. Even if it's extremely painful.* So I do not make a move.

And the pain doesn't disappear. But it stops hurting. Time disappears instead. He and the pain are observed. Like the face of a sleeping baby is observed. Or a mathematical formula written on a piece of paper. Like sheet music. Or like a fire when you can no longer do anything besides watch. The breath is felt inside my body. The air is drawn in through the nose, slightly cooler than the exhale. There's a foot, a hand. A heart that's beating. There's a pain. It's warm. There's a rib cage, rising and falling. There's a serenity that divests me of all my thoughts although they continue to happen. Only there is no Luke.

He gave birth to me correctly. In pain. He is my

third and only parent. He left no commandments but one: that I wouldn't wait to begin living like he did, that I would live. It works out sometimes.

I set up a new email account.

First name: Robert. Last name: Rient.

I ordered business cards: Robert Rient.

I asked my coworkers, friends, and relatives if they'd call me that. They asked why. Because Luke Zamilski died.

Quirky. You want to show off. For publicity. It's silly. Call yourself what you want, but it doesn't make sense. That's sad. Don't say that, I know most certainly he did not die. That's annoying. How fun. Okay, if you want. Come off it.

They have their own idea about me. They have knowledge of me. Greater than my own. Better. It's a knowledge of my body, my inner vision, my memory. My family and close friends sometimes make mistakes. Sometimes they like to call me by Luke's name. Recognition of his death is in itself, after all, acceptance of his death.

There are those who gather evidence. Oh, that's what Luke would've said. Luke is saying that, not you. You acted like Luke, the way I remember. Yes, I collect from those close to me words, gestures, sometimes thoughts, and faith. My therapist looked for split personalities, a rupture, the lack of self-acceptance, trauma. Others invent a third name, a nickname, some kind of bridge between Luke and me.

Most have gotten the hang of it. Few have opted to understand.

In December, a month after returning from the Masurian Lake District, I go on vacation by myself.

The first surprise is a lack of longing for anyone.

The second takes place on the beach. I'm lying there reading when it occurs to me that it's not possible to have been missing out on what I never had in the first place. And then I can't stop laughing. A loud cackle is carried along the sand for several minutes far out to sea. Suddenly it's perfectly clear. I'm laughing at the absurdity of feeling like I've been missing out. Before beginning to miss out on love, money, recognition, reputation, sex, attention, and peace, an expanse opens up. It briefly lingers like the twinkling of an eye. Though the expanse is always there. And in it a place for deciding how I'm supposed to feel with this lack of nothing. Then I can decide on reality. To accept it as singular and complete, or to throw in sadness, worrying, lust, jealousy, gloom, infatuation, in order to feel bad. I'm lying in the same briefs on the beach and I understand that I can't miss out on what I don't have because I don't have it. Any other option is madness, the beginning of a desperate chase.

The third surprise comes a few weeks later. I'm looking in a mirror and it occurs to me that I have never in my life suffered. There is a part of me that has never been hurt by anyone even when it was hit, humiliated, rejected. And that thought triggers a long laugh of years wasted experiencing a phantom pain.

But then I forget. And I start missing what I don't have since I do indeed suffer and I know well my suffering from the past. At this point I'm searching and trusting. Consequently, I fall in love with an idea, a place, a person. I first examine the idea, place, and person of myself. I gladly modify my body and mind in the laboratory. Fortunately, the time it takes for me to stop believing shrinks with each new faith. But I still don't know how to stop looking.

The I really wants me to take part in its drama. The I remembers and worries about the future. The I warns of the danger. The I compares me with others, with how much they have, how quickly they accomplished it, who has heard about them, what they're capable of. In the end the I comes up with solutions to problems that it earlier had brought into existence itself.

Sometimes the I uses faith and it's like an aphrodisiac. Much stronger than any drug. It's like the feeling I've forgotten something important. I return to the place where I forgot, where I lost this idea, convinced that I've lost it in an identifiable place and not inside myself. Sometimes that return helps. Faith sometimes helps.

The I that believes creates palaces in my head. I'll never take up residence in most of them. But it's so good to build them. In the end the I, together with its faith, moves into battle. For success, deliverance, or reprieve. Sometimes it even reaches its designated spot, which it savors. But only for a moment. Success, after all, may be greater. Salvation should be eternal. And a reprieve, more complete. Then others, who I can again compare myself to, appear. A new hunger for recognition appears. And the game starts all over again.

The I doesn't understand the present. It doesn't understand the emptiness that I always feel within myself.

I think about the moment when it happened, when I came into being, as if it were a walk down a train corridor. Luke and I are going in opposite directions. The train is speeding along. Sometimes we lean our hands against a window or a door and we carefully place our steps so as to maintain balance. We look at each other. In a flash we'll meet in the middle of the corridor. That moment is coming. Luke leans back on the windowpane. He takes a step in my direction. I press my head to the glass doors. I look down at my feet so I don't step on Luke. I look up, see his smiling face. At this moment the train lurches, pitching me in his direction. Did the train speed up? I lean my hand against the window so as not to crush Luke. Our temples and cheeks brush against each other for less than a second. But there is enough apparent in this motionless touching to be able to make out that it happened on purpose.

The train rushes on.

I say I'm sorry and continue on in my direction.

Ultimately who I am to you is not who I am.

About the author

Robert Rient is a journalist and a psychologist recommended by the Polish Psychological Association. His work has appeared in Polish publications such as *Charaktery* [Characters], *Coaching, Przekrój* [Cross Section], *Sekrety Nauki* [Secrets of Science], *Sens* [Sense], among others. His novel *It Was About Love* came out in 2013. *Witness* was published in Poland in May 2015.

About the translator

Frank Garrett holds a PhD in philosophy and literary theory. He trained as a translator at the Center for Translation Studies (University of Texas at Dallas) and at Philipps-Universität Marburg after earning advanced certification in Polish philology at the Catholic University of Lublin. In 2001 he was a Fulbright scholar in Warsaw. As an independent philosopher and translator, his work has been published most recently by Black Sun Lit, Duquesne UP, Spurl Editions, and Zeta Books, while his critical reportage has appeared in *3:AM Magazine* and *Transitions Online*. He lives in Dallas with his husband.

Pronunciation Guide

a – as in *father*

ą – (nasal *a*) *on* as in *hone* but without the tongue closing on the *n*; before *b* and *p* it sounds more like *om* as in *home*

b – as in *boy*

c – *ts* as in *cats*

ch – as in Scottish *loch* or German *ach* (can also be pronounced the same as *h*)

cz – *ch* as in *church* (hard *ch*)

ć/ci – *ci* as in *cappuccino* (soft *ch*)

d – as in *dog*

dz – *ds* as in *odds*

dź/dzi – *j* as in *jeans* (soft *j*)

dż – *j* as in *jaw* (hard *j*)

e – as in *egg*

ę – (nasal *e*) *en* as in *hen* but without the tongue closing on the *n*; before *b* and *p* it sounds more like *em* as in *hemlock*; at the end of a word, it tends to lose its nasal quality and sounds more like the Polish *e*

f – as in *fog*

g – as in *go*

h – as in *hall* (can also be pronounced the same as *ch*)

i – *ee* as in *cheek*

j – *y* as in *yes*

k – as in *key*

l – as in *lamp*

ł – *w* as in *wag*

m – as in *man*

n – as in *not*

ń/ni – *ni* as in *onion* or Spanish *ñ* as in *mañana*

o – as in *hope*

ó – *oo* as in *scoot* (pronounced the same as *u*)

p – as in *pup*

r – *rr* as in Spanish *arriba* (trilled, though not as long as in Spanish)

rz – *s* as in *pleasure* (pronounced the same as *ż*) (hard *zh*)

s – as in *say*

sz – *sh* as in *hush* (hard *sh*)

ś/si – *sh* as in *sheep* (soft *sh*)

t – as in *top*

u – *oo* as in *scoot* (pronounced the same as *ó*)

w – *v* as in *vat*

y – as in *myth*

z – as in *zoo*

ź/zi – *ti* as in *equation* (soft *zh*)

ż – *s* as in *pleasure* (pronounced the same as *rz*) (hard *zh*)

Normally, the next-to-the-last syllable is stressed.

Translator's Dedication

I would like to express my gratitude to those who manage and maintain the following web sites and to those who work at the following institutions: Avoid Jehovah's Witnesses (avoidjw. org), Bridwell Library (Perkins School of Theology, SMU), the official Jehovah's Witness site (jw.org), Lochwood Branch Library (Dallas Public Library), the Online Dictionary of JWese (www.answerjw. com/dictionary), and the Watchtower Online Library (wol.jw.org). These archives proved to be invaluable during the countless days of research that this project required.

I also want to thank the following people for their help, support, love, and care over the past several months. This task would have been much more formidable if it were not for Scott Cheshire, Magda Dębowska, Will Evans, Stephen Harding, George Henson, Luz Hernandez, Chris LaFleur, Shayne Larango, Kennan Moore, Marta Morawska, Miguel Murphy, Robert Rient, Jon Roemer, Mariusz Szczygieł, and Jola Zandecki.

I dedicate this translation to Jola, *moja najważniejsza.*

Frank Garrett
June 2016

Translator's Afterword

Polish is a highly inflected language with seven cases and is much more flexible than English, especially in regard to general syntax. In other words, the endings of nouns, pronouns, and adjectives clearly show how those words relate to one another within a sentence despite their order. I tried in my translation to retain some of the complexity from the Polish insofar as it could reasonably sustain meaning as an English sentence. Needless to say, this book was written in a foreign language. But its themes, structure, multiple voices, references to other books, and subject matter also called for a language that is, to borrow one of the author's coined terms, *nadnormalny*, or surnormal. It is neither *out* of the ordinary nor *abnormal* per se and yet this word is perfectly understandable, I think, in both languages.

The very particulars of Luke's life—his Jehovah's Witness upbringing, his homosexuality, his post-communist Polishness—necessarily presented an experience of life that is different from our own; they revealed a self that is otherwise and other than our own. Much like the author's coinages, however, these specifics bear witness to a universality that we foreigners and outsiders of various genders, religious and socio-economic backgrounds, sexualities, and nationalities can nevertheless grasp. His story is, to some extent, our story. As the author wrote, "My unique experiences turn out to be universal." We recognize his longing and his search, we know the ways in which language can shape, contort, and suppress thought, we feel the weight of belonging to an organization no matter its tenets and dogma, and we identify the sites of trauma, even should those sites be labeled with such bizarre names as Szklarska Poręba, Jelenia Góra, or Obrzycko.

Despite the fact that some of the towns and villages mentioned are quite small, most of the geographic place names can indeed be found on a map of southwestern Poland. When so many of these places use the German name in English, since much of this area was part of Germany before World War II, it made no sense to me to try to translate them. Because this is a work of nonfiction, I preserved as many geographic names as possible so that someone could find and trace on a map or in person the locations and sites mentioned. I also retained the abbreviation *ul.* for the Polish *ulica* [street], which appears before street names. Readers seem comfortable enough with the French *rue*, the German *Straße*, and even the Spanish *calle* that this abbreviation shouldn't have posed much of a problem, especially considering that it's the same in most Slavic languages.

I typically think, too, that proper names should be retained as well, particularly in works of nonfiction, memoir, and reportage. The obvious exception in this book is Luke's name (Łukasz). After discussing it with the author, I decided it was more important, instead of a strict adherence to my own preference or to an "accurate" translation (Lucas), to retain the allusion to the biblical Luke, who was this person's namesake. The only other name I translate is Angel's [Anioł]. Other names, most notably Gaja and Inka, could be easily understood, I think, particularly after consulting the pronunciation guide. (*Gaja* would be the equivalent to *Gaia*, or earth; *Inka* would be *Inca* in English—the same word for the pre-Columbian empire that stretched across the western coast of South America.) It should also be noted that many of the people who appeared in the book used a nickname. That is, you won't find too many people officially named Shorty [Niski, Niska] or Bear [Miś].

Even though parts of *Witness* rely so heavily on various books and other material, I limited the amount of citation information in the translation. I also changed the dates of publications mentioned in the Polish to reflect the English language edition I quote from. If there was no parenthetical page number or obvious citation information, then it was either an online or otherwise unpaginated source, or, as is too often the case when dealing with *secret* Jehovah's Witness texts that are impossible to access or no longer available, it was my own translation; that is, I was unable to quote directly from the source text.

Jehovah's Witnesses use a sophisticated vocabulary that will sound foreign to many English speakers, even to—or perhaps especially to—those with a more traditional Protestant background. "Preaching," for example, is what members of the congregation do when they're out knocking on doors or stopping people in public. It is not delivering a *sermon* from the *pulpit* at a *church* on Sunday. Instead, in a Jehovah's Witness context, a *speaker* gives a *speech* from a *platform* in the *hall* to the *preachers* (members of the congregation) during a *meeting*. Not only, then, did I translate this book from Polish, but I translated it into a language that current and former Jehovah's Witnesses would have found familiar and that a larger audience, even those who have no formal religious background or experience, would still have found accessible.

I relied on the 1984 Jehovah's Witness New World Translation of the Holy Scriptures for most of the quoted biblical passages. This would have been the English equivalent of the translation that Luke read and knew during his childhood. Luke's own language would have been seeped in it; his way of thinking would have been shaped by it. (The English translation was revised in 2013.) Most non-Jehovah's Witness readers perhaps noticed just how bizarre the language is in the Jehovah's Witness translation. To say it is flawed and inelegant is an understatement.

When the author mentioned other biblical translations, I either quoted from a readily available English counterpart or I offered my own translation, depending on what the language necessitated. Two Polish biblical translations cited in the text are the Warsaw Bible and the Gdańsk Bible. For the Gdańsk Bible, I cited the

King James. Both are early seventeenth-century translations. Since the Warsaw Bible is a modern Protestant translation from the 1970s, the NIV served as its analog. On one occasion, when the author examined other translations, I brought in the Living Bible (TLB) to show a passage's range of possible meanings and interpretations.

Not only, then, did I place demands upon the reader with strange Polish spellings (in place names and personal names), but I also required a commitment to a religious vocabulary that was strange and to a language that was eccentric. And these demands didn't even address the themes and subject matter of the book itself: drug abuse, mental illness, depression, and dissociative identity disorder, among others.

Thank you for reading.

CPSIA information can be obtained
at www.ICGtesting.com
Printed in the USA
FSOW02n2038200117
29893FS